Praise for *Making a Good Writer Great*

"Linda Seger's new book is an event in Hollywood and in the international film community, a realistic and thought-provoking workbook specifically designed to stimulate the creativity of screenwriters. It will become a classic in the field—guiding writers to bring out the best in their work, which is, after all, Linda Seger's great talent."
—Christopher Vogler, author of *The Writer's Journey: Mythic Structure for Storytellers and Screenwriters*

"Dr. Seger explores the root of all writing—creativity. She fearlessly treads into the depth of writing to affirm your own personal and unique vision. And, I'm quoted in it!"
—David Zucker, writer-director, *The Naked Gun, Airplane!*

"Don't give up! Every writer gets stuck. That's an essential part of the creative process. *Making a Good Writer Great* has terrific, provocative exercises to help you find your way. This book is not a "paint by numbers" screenwriting manual, but instead can help you find and strengthen your own, original voice."
—Karen Croner, screenwriter, *One True Thing*

"Like a steroid for your artistic voice, this practical workbook will boost your confidence, sharpen your writing skills, and help you develop your full creative power."
—David Trottier, author of *The Screenwriter's Bible*

"An outstanding workbook by a gifted writing teacher who clearly shows you the best way to your creative self."
—Cameron West, Ph.D., author of *First Person Plural*

Other books by Linda Seger

Making a Good Script Great
Creating Unforgettable Characters
The Art of Adaptation: Turning Fact and Fiction Into Film
From Script to Screen: The Collaborative Art of Filmmaking
*When Women Call the Shots: The Developing Power and
Influence of Women in Television and Film*

MAKING A GOOD
WRITER GREAT

MAKING A GOOD WRITER GREAT

A Creativity Workbook for SCREENWRITERS

LINDA SEGER

SILMAN-JAMES PRESS ■ LOS ANGELES

First Edition

10 9 8 7 6 5 4 3 2 1

Library of Congress Cataloging-in-Publication Data

Seger, Linda.
Making a good writer great : a creativity workbook for
screenwriters / by Linda Seger. – 1st Silman-James Press ed.
p. cm.
Includes bibliographical references.
1. Motion picture authorship.   2. Television authorship.
I. Title.
PN1996.S3845 1999   808.2'3–dc21   99-33998

ISBN 1-879505-49-5

Cover design by Heidi Frieder

Printed in the United States of America.

SILMAN-JAMES PRESS
1181 Angelo Drive
Beverly Hills, CA 90210

To my dear friends and colleagues
who have deeply touched my creative life:

DARA MARKS
fellow writer, script consultant, seminar leader
who from the beginning embraced my vision,
encouraged me, cared for me, believed in me.
Great woman, Wise woman, Good woman,

and

JUDITH CLAIRE
my miraculous career consultant, who helped me
create, shape, and maintain my business since 1983.
The personification of high ethics, tenderness, and
great love who brings joy and insight into my life.

and

LENNY FELDER
my brilliant book consultant, whose integrity and light
shines through his work and character, who helps shape
my ideas to give them form and clarity and always
believes in me and encourages me.

You have all made me a bigger and better person by
bringing your creative and wonderful selves into my life.

Acknowledgments

Many thanks to my editor, Jim Fox, for his perceptive and detailed work, and to Gwen Feldman, for her support and good work.

Thank you to the many readers who gave me important feedback on the book:

Susie Stroh and Heidi Boyden, who read every chapter several times, did the exercises, struggled with me through the process. My debt to them is enormous.

To Lenny Felder for the titles and for his usual brilliant consulting on my books.

To Sharon Cobb, Sue Terry, Sandi Steinberg, Rachel Ballon, Pamela Jaye Smith, Judith Claire, Cathleen Loeser, Lorene Belisama for reading a number of chapters and guiding me through the difficulties.

And to Anthony Lanza, Dara Marks, Leigh Kennicott, Dr. Jane Hillberry, Lindsay Smith, Anthony Lauro, Janette Dean, Jan Nowina Zarzycki, Bob Hettinger, Carolyn Miller, Ken Unger, Jerry Gillies, Lynn Brown Rosenberg, Ken Wales, Jim Shuman, Shayne Lightner, Margarite Siegel, Loretta Heiser, Dr. Charles Shields, and Barb Van Zuiden for invaluable feedback on individual chapters.

To my sister, Holly Roth, for her support and good work during the editing process.

Always to my very capable assistant, Marsha Parkhill, who keeps me orderly and sane and who gives a spirit of calm to the office.

And to my husband, Peter Hazen Le Var, for affection and care and his sweet love.

Contents

Introduction

During the last twenty years, I've consulted with writers on more than 2,000 scripts. Most of these writers are good. But in the competitive world of TV and film, good is not enough. To sell a script and get the kind of audience reaction you desire, you need to be great.

Whereas *Making a Good Script Great* focused on the craft of screenwriting, this book endeavors to approach the script as the product of the creative process. I believe that great scripts are original, illuminate the complexities of humanity, and resonate with audiences' own personal hopes and struggles. Great scripts don't just happen by luck. They result from a writer's knowledge of craft, unique point of view, and willingness to dig deep into the substance of his or her own life.

This book is designed to help you find and affirm your artistic voice—that special something that makes a script identifiable as uniquely yours. It's about learning to express your creative potential. It's designed to go beyond craft-related principles and into the experience and process of writing. It's to take you beyond simply knowing about writing or being someone who has written a script. It's to take you to that point which allows you to become a great writer.

Can creativity be taught? I believe it can. I believe we are all naturally creative, but somewhere along the way, we became afraid, conventional, unsure of our direction. We need to consciously re-learn and practice what once came naturally to us as children.

Screenwriters need to gain insight into how the creative process works. They need to learn visual thinking and how to work with all the different dimensions that make up a great character. They need to discover how to access their own personal experiences and perceptions and transform them into drama.

How have screenwriters traditionally learned their art? Generally, the new writer begins by thinking up ideas, reading some screenwriting books, maybe taking a seminar or two, and then sitting down and writing one screenplay and then another and then another, often repeating the same mistakes, uncertain about what is missing.

Unaware of their own special gifts, writers sometimes copy the latest hit, but find that it doesn't bring them a sale. Or they write scripts that are innovative, but make no emotional connection with the audience. Either way, talent that could be developed is lost.

If you're already a professional, your inner sense of what works and what doesn't may already be well-trained. But every script is a new beginning and a fresh set of problems. You enter the writing process scared that you might not be able to do it again and knowing that there'll always be at least one unwelcome surprise.

Even when you understand your creative process, you may yearn for some experimentation in your writing but can't break out of your sense of what the industry thinks is commercial. You may no longer want to do the same old thing, but the same old thing has kept you going for some time. You may wonder if, or how, to change. You may feel tired or burned out and want a fresh new direction. New understandings of the creative process can help you tap into your passion and re-vitalize your originality.

This book deals with creativity theories and practices, with an emphasis on practices. The creative process is not just some magical muse that may or may not come to you. She's willing and ready, but you must know how to summon her and welcome her when she arrives.

You can expand your creative powers through very specific techniques. You can activate new parts of your brain, think with more flexibility, be more innovative in your solutions, learn to work with your unconscious to present fresh insights. Instead of writing a good or a pretty good script, you can learn to write a knockout script.

You can do the exercises in this book alone as part of a daily ritual. You can do these exercises with a partner. Or you can work in a group, sharing your discoveries with other creative minds.

Since this is a book about creativity, you needn't be conventional about how you work with it. Feel free to skip around. Read back to front if you want. Some exercises will affirm what you're already doing. Others will open your mind to different approaches.

As you read this book and do its exercises, I hope that you'll have fun, be delighted, be engaged, and be fulfilled. This book is the head brought together with the heart—the craft with the art, the knowledge with the experience. Your journey should be one of discovery and delight.

1.

Building a Strong Foundation for Your Creative Work

You're a writer. A writer writes. That doesn't mean you don't struggle, procrastinate, feel insecure, wonder what to do next, feel confused and uncertain, and ask yourself if what you've written is worth anything. But you write anyway. You write because you have something to say. You write because you have stories pushing at you. You write because you have characters aching to get out. You write because you have ideas that matter. You write because you have a burning desire to tell the truth.

If your passion is great enough, no one can keep you from your work. You need no special tools—just something to write with, something to write on, something to write about. You need no special location. Writing can be done anywhere, under all circumstances. Writers have written in prisons and concentration camps, while dying of hunger, while suffering subzero temperatures, while trapped in caves and on deserted islands. They've written in the daytime, after work, and in the dark hours of the night, scribbling their thoughts by flashlight. They've written on planes, trains, and automobiles. On ships and at writers' retreats.

The need to communicate with audiences, to move one's thoughts from the inner stirrings of the soul out through the fingers, can't be stopped.

Being a writer demands a missionary's zeal, a desire that won't let you go. But you need something more. To be merely competent or even good is not enough.

Most of my writing clients are smart. They're disciplined. They know all the basics. Some even have marketable ideas. But there's a good chance that many of them won't make it. Why? Because many of them don't understand the creative process. They work against the creative process rather than making friends with it. They work when they're creatively stale. They wait for inspiration, rather than make inspiration. They get frustrated, trying to force the creative process because they don't know when to work and when to wait. They give up too soon, not realizing that re-doing, re-thinking, re-writing, and re-figuring are all part of the writing process.

Creativity is not as magical and mystical as you might think. Certain techniques, exercises, practices, ways of working can help your creativity flow, get you unstuck when you're stuck, and help you build on your natural talents to lead you to being the great writer who creates great scripts.

Is This Book for You?

Do you ever feel stuck? Do your ideas fail to flow? Do you have trouble figuring out what to write next? Do you ever wonder if you should give up?

Do you feel a passion for your ideas but find they keep coming out mushy and unclear?

Do you have trouble getting into a writing schedule?

Do you have trouble making your script visual and cinematic?

Do you have trouble creating vibrant, unforgettable characters?

Do you sometimes wonder how creative you are? whether you're good enough? Do you wonder if there's any way to become more creative? Do you wonder if, just maybe, you could become a great writer?

If you answered "yes" to any of these questions, then you should ask yourself:

Am I you willing to learn?

Am I willing to work at my writing?

Am I willing to begin a daily writing discipline?

If you are, and if you commit to working with this book for three to six months, I guarantee that your creative process will serve you. Once it does, your writing will be more vibrant, your characters deeper, your stories richer.

Do you really want to write?

THINK ABOUT

Why do you write? What drives you?
What makes it worthwhile?

I write because I _____.
Writing my last script was worthwhile
because _____.
The fun of writing happens when _____.
In spite of the struggle, I'm willing to keep writing
because _____.

THINK ABOUT

Why don't you write? What hinders you?
What are your fears and resistances?
I'm afraid to write because _____.

I have trouble getting started because _____.
My worst fears about writing are _____.

Many writers have said to me, "I can't get started" or "I can't find the time to write" or "I'd like to be a writer, but I haven't written anything for years." I generally answer, "If you want to write, write." No one is telling you that you must be a writer. There are plenty of writers around to more than feed the need for the written word. The only reason to write is because you need to and want to.

This book is about finding your own unique voice so that what you create has your own personal stamp upon the work. It's about expressing your identity through *what* you write and *how* you write.

As you work through this book, you'll find warm-up exercises, practice exercises, and exercises designed for your current script. The following is an exercise that Karen Croner, writer of *One True Thing*, shared with me. It is designed specifically for when you begin to work on a script.

> Write a letter to yourself about why you love the idea for your script. Rave about how wonderful the script will be. Go on and on about why producers will want to buy it and audiences will flock to see it. Talk about why the writing is so terrific, how dimensional the characters are, what a unique piece of work it is. Then seal the letter and put it away. We'll come back to this letter in a later chapter.

The Creative Process

Many new writers believe that the creative process is all about magic. The Muse pops out now and then, teases you a bit, and then disappears. Not necessarily. Some writers believe it's all about talent. They think they have some, but the great writers have more of it. Not always. Some writers believe that they struggle but the great writers do not. Not true.

How are the great writers able to keep coming up with new ideas? Of course, some of it is talent—and every reader of this book has some of that. But much of it is also about knowing techniques that feed and activate the creative process.

What is creativity? Creativity is the ability to come up with original work.

The journey from an idea to a final work is not one act, but a process. In 1926, psychologist Graham Wallas defined the stages of the creative process as preparation, incubation, illumination, and verification. Other studies add memory and problem-definition to this list.

The process moves from producing a germ of an idea to fleshing it out to outlining it to writing various drafts of it to finally getting it out there. Along the way, you'll work and wait and struggle. Everything will flow for a bit, and then you'll wait again and you'll work some more. And then ideas will come, and later, they won't come. It sounds haphazard and chaotic. It is. But it also has discipline and predictability and clarity. As you move through the process, you'll encounter some stages a number of times. It's not a neat, linear flow—the process circles around, repeating each step a number of times.

Remembering

The writer never creates out of nothing. While many writers begin the process with research, along the way, most writers will rely on their memory of stories, feelings, and experiences to shade their work and make it accessible to others.

Remembering often begins with memories of childhood. Poet Rainer Maria Rilke said that memories and dreams are inexhaustible resources for the writer. Remember. Remember when. Remember long days spent dreaming about what might be. Remember running, playing hide-and-seek, and yelling and screaming with the neighbor kids. Remember the feelings of being left out, alienated. Remember times when you felt scared. Remember the experience of doing anything or feeling anything for the first time.

Remembering is a creative act. When you're able to bring an experience to life through a script, the audience understands its authenticity. If you made it ring true, they'll live it, feel it, sense it.

Part of your creative work is sharpening your powers of memory: to hear the sounds, to evoke the mood, to remember the pain. Thomas Wolfe calls it "making a living out of the substances of one's own life."[1]

All through this book, you'll be using your memories to help you get at the unexpected shock of truth. You'll build on your personal memories to make your characters and situations feel authentic.

REMEMBER

Start a journal or notebook just for memories.
Start with the first 10 years of your life. Then move from decade to decade, trying to capture events and experiences and people who were part of your world. What are the sounds of childhood? The dialogue? The shouts and screams and rowdy behavior? The murmurs of quiet play?

What were the most profound scenes from your childhood? The most exciting? The most abusive? The scariest? Write them down. Try to capture emotions as well as events.

What was your most frustrating experience? When were you most content? Write out the high and low emotional moments: The times when you sobbed from fear or frustration. The times you laughed the loudest and longest. The moments you glowed with love and accomplishment.

ORGANIZE

Start a file folder and label it "children's memories." Start another one for "children's dialogue." You might want to include photos and drawings that capture your images of childhood. Next time you write a script that includes children, you'll already have usable information to help you capture the scene.

DISCUSS

Talk to friends and relatives about their memories. If you're working with a partner or in a writing group, try working off of each other's childhood experiences, combining elements to create a scene. You may take your character, combine it with another person's situation, use some of another's dialogue. Memory will ground the experience, giving it depth and weight.

REFLECT

Could any of these scenes be used in a film?

CREATE

Create a scene based on your memories.

Integrate Your Memory With Your Script

If you are currently working on a script, work with the memories implicit in your story.

YOUR SCRIPT

What in your script relies on your memories of events and emotions? Write about those memories to see if they give you ideas about how to further layer and shade your work.

Preparation

Creativity often begins with memories that join with imagination and ideas from other sources to form complex combinations. According to writer Arthur Koestler, the more unusual the combination, the more creative it is.

Creativity comes from a collision of ideas that might not ordinarily be thought of as fitting together. The "Ah ha!" the "Eureka!" the "I get it!" only comes when enough unique ideas have been pulled together.

Arthur Koestler, in his classic work *The Act of Creation*, compares the creative act's "ah ha" with the moment when we get a joke's punchline.[2] Maybe you've heard this classic screenwriter joke.

"How many writers does it take to change a lightbulb?"

The writer answers, "Why does it need changing?"

If you laughed, a collision of unlike ideas occurred. You brought together two different frames of reference—the world of lightbulb jokes and the knowledge that writers don't want to change their work. If you didn't know about lightbulb jokes or the writer's desire to guard every word, you wouldn't get it.

The next joke is about producers. The laugh depends upon another frame of reference—the producer's response to the writer's work.

"How many producers does it take to change a lightbulb?"

The producer answers, "Why does it have to be a lightbulb?"

You get the joke if you understand that producers, by nature, always want to make changes. A producer often asks: "Why does it have to be a female lead?" "Why does it have to be set in Detroit?" "Why does it have to be a comedy at all?"

To further understand this idea, think about an extremely creative movie you've seen. What unlike ideas had to come together to make it a unique work? Perhaps you thought of the combination of a contemporary war movie, shot in black and white, with a man who doesn't admit his goodness (*Schindler's List*). Or a chase movie where both the cat and the mouse are the good guys (*The Fugitive*). The greatest writer in the world has writer's block (*Shakespeare in Love*). Television and reality are the same, except one person doesn't know it (*The Truman Show*). Each great script combines hundreds of unique ideas.

Force a Relationship to Occur

Your script becomes original when it's a unique combination of events, characters, images, ideas, and storylines. In the following exercises, you're going to force your mind into this type of creative mode.

Create a story by combining the following elements:
The song "Three Blind Mice"
The murder of a Secret Service agent
A Chinese megalomanic

You can see this connection in the James Bond film *Dr. No*. Consider this combination:

> A young woman with a retarded brother.
> A boyfriend with zits.
> A dog that won't let go.

There's Something about Mary, written by Ed Decter, John J. Strauss, Peter Farrelly, and Bobby Farrelly.

Here are some new ones. See if you can form a story or a scene or a character from the following three unlike combinations:

> a character who collects pre-Colombian art
> a boat race
> linguini with marinara sauce

> rounding up cattle
> talking about religion
> playing the flute

> fixing the computer
> dancing around the Maypole
> training a cat

Notice how your mind reaches to make these connections. Part of the creative side of preparation is playing around with ideas. Looking for possibilities. Fitting together things that, at first glance, don't appear to belong together. To the creative mind, it's all possible.

To create, something needs to be inside your mind. You have to prepare, to fill your mind, to immerse yourself in your subject so a unique combination can occur. Knowledge is an essential first step in the creative process.

Know Your Domain

Preparation means learning about your field, your arena, your domain, which usually occurs over a long period of time. As a screenwriter, your domain is film or television writing. If you don't know it, you can't write it.

I've known writers who want to write for television, but don't watch it. They know nothing about the shows on the air, what the networks are looking for, or who their audience is for their script.

I've had clients who write features, but never go to movies.

To create a unique work, you need to build on what has gone before. Without knowing the domain, one is apt to come up with the same old ideas, or with ideas that don't fit the medium and therefore can't find a buyer or an audience. Your ideas might seem creative to you, but others who know the domain might say, "We already did that," or "We thought of that already; it didn't work," or "It might work for a novel, but it's definitely not a screenplay."

As a writer, your domain includes the craft of writing. If you're reading this book, you're doing preparation by learning your craft and discovering your art. Taking seminars, participating in writing workshops, going to conferences are all part of the preparation necessary to become a better writer.

Chances are, you've already put in some years preparing.

THINK

Make a list of what you have done so far to learn your craft:
What classes have you taken?
What books have you read?
Have you worked with a writing group?
Have you read scripts to understand script format and the "feel" of a great script?
How long have you been writing? How many stories have you written?
What have you learned from watching film and TV?

To be a great screenwriter, you will need to understand the following concepts. Where these concepts are discussed in this book is shown in parentheses.

The craft of storytelling (Chapter Four).

How to work with ideas dramatically (Chapter Five).

Becoming a visual- and sensation-thinker (Chapter Six).

Getting in touch with your unconscious (Chapters Seven and Eight).

How to work with oppositional thinking (Chapter Nine).

How to create dimensional characters (Chapter Nine).

Your domain is not just the domain of screenwriting in general, but the domain of a particular genre. Many writers begin by experimenting with different genres in order to find their voices, sometimes writing a thriller, a comedy, a horror, a sci-fi, and a soap. Although this can be one way to find your voice and see which you prefer, it's almost impossible to learn all the underlying rules and concepts of such diverse genres. Once you find a genre you like, you'll need to study it and write several scripts in that genre to master it.

Of course, writers can easily become stereotyped and trapped into such roles as terrific comedy writer or master of the sex sizzler. This isn't all bad. Hollywood recognizes those writers who are masters of a genre, and is more apt to buy their scripts than those of writers who keep changing genres.

How long does it take to master your craft? The correct answer is "forever," but there's a more concrete answer too. Psychologist John Hayes recounts studies done to learn when famous painters, composers, and poets did their most creative work. In most cases, the artist's significant creative work was produced after at least five to ten years of preparation.[3] These statistics reinforce my own observations from working with more than 2,000 writers. Most writers will have their first option or sale of a script after five years or after writing four or five scripts. The option may be for only $1,000 (or may even be a free option), but it's a beginning. Several writers I know received their big break on their eighth or ninth script, which made them a "hot item" in Hollywood. But the great work—the mastery of the field— takes more years to achieve. Even the tremendously successful Steven Spielberg played around with film for years before his first break into commercial films. His first big success, *Jaws*, threatened to be his first big failure because they couldn't get the shark to work. And it took about twenty movies and twenty-five years before he won his Academy Award for *Schindler's List*.

Many are appalled by these statistics, but the statistics tell the truth—great work does not happen without years of preparation.

Do not despair because you haven't sold your first script or won an Academy Award for your second. All those successful people whom you envy aren't just lucky. They've spent years learning the craft and finding their voices as artists. I started writing when I was ten, wrote my first and only novel at the age of thirteen, and wrote stories and essays and articles for more than thirty years before my first book was published. Looking back, I had no idea that all of that playing around was preparation for my work as a non-fiction writer.

Knowledge does not derive only from reading and attending classes and watching tons of films. Knowledge gained this way can be too linear and repetitive—going down the same track, taking one class after another after another, watching one film after another, writing and rewriting and rewriting, without any clear idea of what you're writing and why. Rather than expanding and developing your abilities, you simply repeat what has gone before.

Linear knowledge can lay the groundwork for non-creative thought because creativity is often circular or takes leaps in logic. If all you have in your mind is how every-one has done it before you, your mind will have trouble making creative leaps.

Think instead of learning your craft through a series of related, but not necessarily linear, activities. Think of a circle, not of a line.

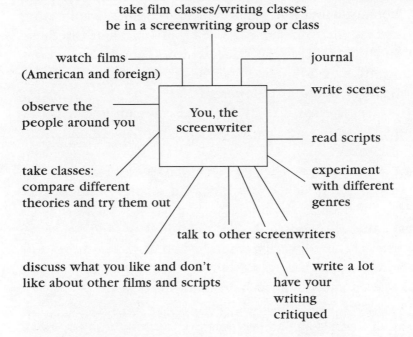

take film classes/writing classes
be in a screenwriting group or class

watch films
(American and foreign)

journal

write scenes

observe the
people around you

You, the
screenwriter

read scripts

take classes:
compare different
theories and try them out

experiment
with different
genres

talk to other screenwriters

discuss what you like and don't
like about other films and scripts

write a lot
have your
writing
critiqued

CONSIDER

What other knowledge or experience do you think you still need in order to have some mastery over your work?

BRAINSTORM

Make a list of the subject matter where you already have done significant preparation and would be able to write a script about that topic with very little research.

Some of my clients are doctors who write medical stories. Some are real estate agents whose main characters sell real estate. Some are lawyers who write about lawyers. Some are musicians who incorporate music into their scripts. Though you may have only begun to write, you undoubtedly have considerable knowledge in some area—in child-rearing or college life or working in a video store. That is all potentially valuable preparation already completed.

Explore. Interact. Experience.

You prepare to write by being curious and aware. You prepare by taking notes about what you observe. You're probably a people-watcher, maybe even an eavesdropper. Maybe you're just plain nosy. You follow the O.N.E. Principle—Observe. Notice. Experience.

Decide to do more:

Be nosier.

Observe more.

Be Curious-er.

Look. Ask questions.

Get in the habit of trying to see and understand something new every day.

Preparation demands you have tools, such as notebooks—lots of them. Like an artist who is always sketching, you need to capture dialogue, the interesting character models, unusual images. You may want to have notebooks by your bed, in your car, and in your purse and briefcase.

You prepare for a specific script through research—visiting libraries, interviewing people to learn about a job or a situation, putting yourself into a situation to understand all its details.

This preparation could entail overcoming a shyness or fear that people won't want to answer your questions or will think you're prying. But most people are happy to answer your questions about their jobs, their children, what they feel and think and why. If you approach them in an open, non-judgmental manner, they'll thank you for allowing them to share what they think. And if all else fails, you can always say, "I'm writing a major motion picture about some-one like you. May I ask you some questions?"

CONSIDER

Would you like to research some vocations as possible jobs for a character?
Rock-climbing? Orchid-growing? Saxophone-playing?

THINK ABOUT

How would you research? Go to the library? Talk to people? Hang out with them? Read books? Watch videos? Attend conferences? All of the above?

YOUR SCRIPT

If you're already working on a script, do you need to do additional preparation about subject matter, character, context, vocabulary?

Do a New-Experience Exercise

The following is an exercise I've used with a number of writing groups—always with amazing results. It's designed to take you through a number of stages of the creative pro-cess within a short amount of time.

STEP ONE

Within the next few weeks, do something you've never done before. You might go to a country-western dance or an auction, take a flying lesson, serve soup at a homeless shelter, go to an upscale boutique and try on clothes. You might ride along with the police. You might take a gliding lesson or a piano lesson. Or volunteer at a hospital. Choose anything that interests you and is new to you.

STEP TWO

Find out at least five or ten pieces of information that you would never have known if you had not undertaken this experience. In the soup kitchen, find out the quantity of food they need, how they order, the equipment they need. In the gliding lesson, learn about updrafts and foot pedals and the names of the parts of the plane and how to get speed from the plane. If you go skiing, find out the brands of ski boots, the particular names of ski runs, such as Suicide Run. Learn what's the "in" brand of ski clothes.

Art is in the details. Observe. Notice. Experience.

STEP THREE

As soon as your experience is over, write it down exactly as it happened. The dialogue, the look of the place, how many people were there, what they were wearing, any conflicts you noticed, where the power structure was.

STEP FOUR

Write how you felt: Uncomfortable? Excited? Anxious? Irritated? Afraid? Explore. Gush out your feelings on the page.

STEP FIVE

Look at what you've written. Did you capture the experience? What's good about it? Would it be more dramatic if you changed it? If it needs changing, reshape it to add sizzle, without compromising the truth you discovered through the experience.

STEP SIX

Create several scenes based on what you've written above. Add more characters. Create a different conflict. Relocate the scene. Combine characters. Create a conflict. Change the dialogue. Add a bad guy. Add a good guy. Imagine possibilities.

STEP SEVEN

Share your scene with a friend, a writing partner, or a writing group. Do they feel you captured the experience on the page? Did they learn anything surprising and new from your experience?

This is an exercise you can do over and over again to reshape your experience into dramatic form.

How much preparation do you need? Think, for instance, about a script that required considerable research—such as *Rain Man*. Writers Barry Morrow and Ron Bass had to find out about autism—what it was, how it worked psychologically, how much you could communicate with an autistic person, what an autistic person could and couldn't do. They had to discover how the brilliance of the autistic savant would express itself.

They then had to re-shape their research into dramatic form. Notice that there are no scenes in the film where research comes out as research. Doctors don't give lectures on the autistic savant. There are no boring passages filled with information. How do we learn about it? Through action. A waitress drops a box of toothpicks and Raymond glances at the hundred or so on the floor and tells her there are 142.

How many interviews would a writer need to do to find such a telling detail that dramatically defines autism?

How creative would a writer need to be to render a scene so succinctly?

YOUR SCRIPT

What needs to be researched in your script? Put yourself in the experience. Write the scene. Reshape the scene to fit your script.

You've researched. You've prepared. You've remembered emotions, experiences, and stories. You've begun to integrate them with your script. But maybe the ideas aren't yet clicking. You're not sure what to do. Now you're ready for the next stage of the creative process—waiting.

2.

Finding Out What Fuels Your Most Productive Writing

When I was writing this book, I spoke about the creative process with several great writers—writers who wrote critically and commercially acclaimed films, who had been nominated for awards, who had long and successful writing careers.

I also spoke to a number of good writers, some of whom were on the way to being great. I noticed one major difference between the great and the good. The great writers knew how to feed their process. They knew when to let their ideas sit and simmer and when to prod their process to keep the ideas flowing. They knew what worked for them and what didn't. They were both more disciplined and more spontaneous. They were able to use their creative process to keep writing on a daily schedule to meet deadlines, to come up with solutions even when they might have drawn a complete blank hours before. All the great writers had a number of techniques they found helpful, some of which were used by many, others that were quite unique.

Many good writers may know technique but have no patience. They force the creative process. When they do, what they create can be stale and predictable. The good writers hoped the flow would happen and stopped writing when it didn't. Or they tried to push it, but got nothing.

REFLECT

What do you already know about your creative process? Describe it. How does it work? When does it work well? When does it seem not to work at all?

Discovering Your Creative Time

Each writer has times of the day when the creative process flows best and times when it just seems stuck or slow-moving. You need to value your creative time and make sure that nothing interferes with it if you want to be a disciplined, creative, and prolific writer. Since I'm a morning writer, I rarely schedule a breakfast or even a lunch meeting. Other morning writers I know turn on the answering machine until 2:00 p.m. or get up at 5:00 a.m. to make sure they encounter no distractions for several hours.

EXPERIMENT

Every day, write something about whatever interests you—write about your childhood, about your newest project, about your dreams, about how you feel, about yesterday's experiences. What you write about doesn't matter. For the first week, write in the morning for at least half an hour, longer if possible. See how the writing flows. Next week, write in the evening. The following week, write in the afternoon.

REFLECT

When did your writing flow the best? When did you
feel the freshest? When were you the most original?
When were you the most excited about your work?

I have known very few afternoon writers—most of us
find that our minds are better for editing rather than creative writing in the afternoon. But TV writer Michael Zagor
told me that he once went to an educational psychologist
when he was creatively stuck. The psychologist noticed he
wrote the most between 11:30 and 1:00 and 3:30 and 6:00.
"I get it," he said, "I write when I'm hungry!"

Make no judgments about when you're supposed to
write. There's no room for "supposed tos" in this part of
the process. That might come later, when a producer tells
you you're supposed to deliver your screenplay next week
to get the $50,000 bonus. That's an all right "supposed to"—
but don't worry about that yet.

Once you know your best writing time, treasure it, cherish it, guard it, and don't let anything interfere with it. This
might mean that some mornings you'll wake up at 3:00 a.m.
and get out of your warm covers to write down something
that will disappear if you don't make the sacrifice. It might
mean that you need to turn off your telephone and let your
answering machine take over during your peak writing
time. Some writers put on a timer, making sure that nothing interferes with the time they've set aside to work.

Once you've experienced your best times for writing,
start experimenting with how long you can write before
you get tired and the Muse goes underground. Academy
Award-winning writer Frank Pierson (*Dog Day Afternoon*)
writes from ten a.m. to noon every day. That's his writing
time. I usually write three hours a day, unless deadlines
loom. Some writers, such as novelists Robin Cook and

Nancy Taylor Rosenberg, write ten to fifteen hours a day.
But that's unusual.

> For the next few days, tell the Muse that you'd like
> your creativity to flow, and ask her to stop by. Have
> your notebook handy and agree to write whenever
> the spirit moves you, whatever time of the day or
> night. Keep track of when she comes to you.
>
> Next time you have trouble getting an idea, repeat
> whatever activity seems to reinforce your Muse,
> whether it's walking, gardening, sleeping…

Defining the Problem

Once you know your most creative time, you may find that
you start to write but seem to get nowhere. You're trying
to work something out, you have a feeling for where you
want to go, but you can't figure out how to get from a
muddy idea to a clear script. You may need to start by defining the problem.

Creation begins with the desire to change something,
to make it better, to resolve a problem, to take care of a
need. Great creative work depends on the ability to define
what it is you're looking for. Solutions flow from clear problem definitions.

Defining the problem demands clarifying your intention.
If you define the problem as, "I have to write a script of
120 pages that will make a lot of money," you aren't apt to
achieve much. But if you phrase it as, "I want to do a horror film, but I want it also to be really funny without compromising the terror. How will I pull it off?" you'll find that
your creative mind will seek answers to your question.

Without specificity, your creative process has nothing
to chew on. But by defining the two ideas (horror and

comedy) that you need to combine in unique ways, your mind begins its process toward the ah-ha experience. If the ah-ha isn't forthcoming, you may need to feed yourself more ideas. This could mean further research or exploring and playing around with new ideas until something starts to sizzle. You could watch horror films that are funny and analyze how they achieve humor. Think about horrific experiences in your own life or in your dreams that have a humorous bent to them and explore them in a journal. When all else fails, you can summon the Muse from your unconscious, asking her to think up some funny horror moments. Then go to sleep and wait for the Muse to come along.

Notice

The more knowledgeable you are about the craft of screenwriting, the easier it will be to define the problem. The more specific the problem-definition, the more able you are to create unique solutions.

YOUR SCRIPT

What is the problem you're trying to solve in your writing? Phrase it as clearly as possible. Put it aside. And wait.

Incubation

Incubating ideas is one of my favorite parts of the process. I only have to wait. In fact, the incubation phase demands you do everything except write.

Once ideas start floating around in your mind, they will automatically churn and search for new connections. Let them do their work while you take a break. Part of the creative process is doing something else while allowing your Muse to work unconsciously.

In our rational, conscious lives, we move in a linear, chronological fashion. B follows A, C follows B. It's one-dimensional, straightforward, clear and concise. However, the creative unconscious does not resolve problems through a linear model, but through circling around.

"When we think consciously about an issue, our previous training and the effort to arrive at a solution pushes our ideas into a linear direction usually along predictable or familiar lines," says psychologist Mihaly Csikszentmihalyi. If the ideas come, they're obvious and predictable. But by waiting, allowing the unconscious to incubate and play around with the ideas, "Ideas can combine and pursue each other every which way. Because of this freedom, original connections that would be at first rejected by the rational mind have a chance to become established."[1]

Creative people seem to be able to control this restructuring. How do they do that? By being willing to wait.

What do you do while waiting? Writer David Klass (*Desperate Measures*) says that when you hit a snag, "The worst thing to do is to sit and look at the computer. Instead, I play competitive sports, see a good or bad movie, or swim. I let the problem work itself out. Rather than trying to intellectually figure it out, I trust that if I step away, it will sort itself out."

While waiting, do anything that is not writing—swim, drive, garden, weave, play piano, run, or walk.[2] When you focus on a physical or sensory experience, another part of your brain can pursue new associations and new orderings.[3]

Some creative artists recommend taking frequent showers and baths during the incubation period. No, not because creative writing makes you work up a sweat, but because many good ideas come when you're alone, away from distraction, and with the soothing sounds of water. Alan Kay, who helped develop the personal computer, said he got his be>. ideas when showering. He asked his company to install a shower in his office so he could shower every time he got stuck. They refused. He estimates they lost millions of dollars as a result.[4]

QUESTION

What activities help trigger your creative process?

The secret to this waiting period is to have other things to do, but always have a notebook nearby. You don't know when the Muse will pop up. The Muse doesn't keep normal working hours. She gets little sleep and seems to have no respect for your sleep habits. My Muse loves to wake me up with lots of great ideas around 3:00 a.m. I've learned to humorously say, "You've got to be kidding!" Then I get out my notebook and start writing.

Once she pops up, be ready. Writer-director Anthony Minghella (*The English Patient, Truly Deeply Madly*) says that when the Muse is working, the experience is almost like taking dictation. He sees his script as already finished, but locked in his desk drawer. Sometimes the Muse gives him the key, he opens the drawer and starts copying what's there. Sometimes the drawer only opens for a few minutes, and he has to be quick about it. When she comes, don't ignore her. She brings the ultimate gift—creativity.

Awakening the Muse

Sometimes the Muse needs to be prodded. Many of the best writers I know have techniques for summoning her.

1

My writing friend Sharon Cobb, who recently sold a project to Fox 2000, takes what she calls a story nap. Whenever she can't think of how the next scene starts or how to resolve a specific problem, she writes a question on a pad

("How does the next scene begin?" or "What does Charlie do to convince Grace that he loves her?" etc.) She then lies down and always finds that ideas flow within twenty minutes. She invites the Muse by asking a question that the Muse can't resist answering.

2

When I'm stuck, this is an exercise I often do that always yields results: Before you go to bed, write down a definition of the problem that you're trying to solve. Be as specific as possible. If you don't get an answer by morning, stay in bed until you do. If you still don't get an answer after five or ten minutes, roll over and doze for a bit. If that doesn't work, lie on your back and think about the problem. Have a notebook and a tape recorder by your bed so you can capture the answer quickly. I notice that lying on my left side (the more intuitive side) is most likely to yield creative answers. Experiment with this. I've used this technique a number of times and never stayed in bed more than half an hour before coming up with an answer.

3

Writer Linda Woolverton (*Beauty and the Beast*) uses a similar technique. She takes a "thinking walk" and tells herself that she's not allowed to come home until she's figured out the scene.

4

Write a note that defines the problem and asks for help. Novelist Sue Grafton, who writes the Kinsey Milhone mysteries, writes little notes to her right brain. Here's an example:

March 25, 1992
Dear RB (Right Brain),
Please use your massive intelligence, wit, and ingenuity to come up with some sparkling twist or device to give "J" lift. It wouldn't hurt my spirits either while you're at it...
Thanks.
Your pal,
Sue[5]

5

If you're spiritual, write a note to God, defining the problem, expressing your concern, and promising to get up in the middle of the night if an answer is given.

Remember that the Holy Spirit is also a creative spirit.

6

Try deliberately waking up in the middle of the night and writing while you're sleepy. Set your alarm if necessary. Or, if you just happen to wake up, even if you don't have any ideas, write.

7

Use writing warm-ups to get your ideas flowing. John Steinbeck warmed up by writing a letter to his editor each morning. He explained the work he was going to do that day, the problems he was trying to resolve, and how he was thinking and feeling about the book. When he was sufficiently warmed up, he stopped the letter and began writing the book.

8

Change locations. I wrote part of a chapter of *When Women Call the Shots* sitting on the floor of the busy Beijing, China, airport with my arms and legs looped through all my valuables—purse, backpack, suitcase.

When I was teaching in Sweden, I spent a weekend by a lake, writing at a picnic table. I wrote several first drafts of chapters for this book at the Pikes Peak Writer's Retreat.

I've written in the office, at Ruby's 1950's restaurant, and stopped alongside the road. Take your notebook on walks and hikes, on planes and trains. Keep some paper with you in church. Plenty of ideas have come during a boring sermon and even a very good one. Abraham Lincoln wrote the Gettysburg Address on a train. In your own home or apartment, move from one room to another.

9

Visualize the idea you're after. Draw diagrams or flow charts that show the action of the characters as they move throughout the story—city to country, around the center of town, or even around the bedroom for the love scene. Storyboard the scene to help you imagine what the audience will see. Draw arrows and graphs and funny looking houses and cars to see the movement of the story. As a script consultant, I use colored pencils and pens to graph the intersection of plots and subplots to help the writer see what's happening in a script. The colored pens and magic markers bring a magical, playful, spontaneous quality to the work.

10

Watch a movie that has some similarity to your script in terms of genre, style, story, character, theme, location, or context. Your mind will automatically connect your story and the film, looking for new associations. You can do this same exercise by walking around when you're stuck and telling yourself that you want your mind to find some symbol that will lead you to a solution.

11

One of the script consultants whom I trained in Stockholm, Ingeborg Torgeson, recommends looking at photos or post-cards or paintings and asking yourself, "Which of these is most like what I want in my story?"

12

Ask "What if?" to allow your mind to be flexible. What if your main character were female rather than male? What if your story took place in Detroit, not Miami? What if you added comedy to the story? What if you started your story thirty pages later?

13

Purposely add distractions to your work—turn on the television or write in the middle of kids and cats and stereos and ringing telephones. For some people, distractions actually make their minds focus better.

14

Writer Karen Croner recommends writing down the worst ideas you can think of. Once they're written, you'll find they aren't as bad as you thought. Or you might find getting them down gets you over your procrastination or your judgment that you're going to do a terrible job. Once the worst ideas are on the page, it can only get better.

15

Australian writer Karen Altmann gave me the following exercise:

Buy some cheap notepads. On the first piece of note paper, write down an idea, or a scene, or sketch out a character, or an image. Put it face down. On the following sheets of paper, repeat the process with different ideas, scenes, character sketches, or images. Tear the sheets off, place them face down. Don't judge. Don't worry if they don't make sense. Just get it out.

Suppose you're writing an action-adventure script that takes place in Turkey and you're stuck. Start writing—anything:

Ancient talisman smuggled out of Turkey.

Put it face down, and go to the next one.

Getaway train ride.

Place it face down. Go to the next one.

The turbulent sea.
Minarets at sunset.
Guy has a pet rabbit. Dialogue about Turkish coffee.

Give yourself a goal—to fill up at least fifty notepads with whatever comes to your mind. Then go back and see if anything is usable. Chances are, some of it is.

You are not making any judgment on these ideas. You are simply trying to write down as many ideas as quickly as possible to free your mind and make your thinking as flexible as possible.

YOUR SCRIPT

Are you stuck in any part of your script? If so, start writing down any ideas that pop into your head, brilliant or stupid. Do not evaluate your ideas until you have at least thirty or fifty of them.

The answers to your script, story, or character problems may be in your unconscious mind. They may have gone underground. They may seem inaccessible. When this happens, decide NOT to approach them consciously, but let your unconscious mind chew on them for a while. Do everything except write.

If you find you're not writing at all, you're spending too much time in the incubation process. At that point, you may need to admit you're stuck or procrastinating or afraid or your unconscious may be telling you that writing is not your thing.

If so, force yourself to write at least twenty minutes a day for five days straight. If you find no joy in the activity, change professions. But if it was only fear holding you back, by writing you should soon find your ideas taking you into the next stage of the process.

Illumination

You've suddenly got it. Ideas come rapidly with a clarity of thought, with insight, with the right words. This is the ah-ha moment that depends on your preparation and incubation. The illumination experience seems to exist outside the realm of time. Yesterday, you spent two hours trying to write a page and, suddenly, within three hours, you've written ten pages that are far superior in quality to anything that has gone before.

You need to catch it when it comes. That means knowing techniques that help you get it down and organize it.

Getting It Down, Keeping It Flowing

Great writers use a variety of techniques to work with the Muse.

My friend Sharon Cobb is one of the most organized writers I know: "I have dozens of file folders. One section is labeled 'Characters' and consists of twelve to fifteen files, including character names, antagonist, comedy characters, character behavior, character motivations, physical descriptions, possessions, psychological disorders. I then have a section labeled 'Future Projects,' which includes twelve to fifteen files of ideas, labeled by genre, for future scripts. Another folder is called 'Movie Titles,' where I collect title ideas. I have crime files, such as on murder, criminals, police procedures, etc. I also have a directing notebook with images I like, and sometimes will even include a photograph or picture.

"I also have a section where I break down, minute by minute, the structure of films. Before I write a new genre, I'll break down three of the best films in that genre to analyze why these particular films work so well. I want to know where the comedy is, how long the scenes are, how often the antagonist appears, how the writer achieved tension and suspense, how the scene sequences work, and then I also analyze the individual characters. This is analytical and mechanical, simply to know how the film works and why.

"When I get a lot of ideas on one project, I start a notebook for that script, using dividers to separate characters, outlines, possible scenes, etc.

"At one point, I found the file folders got out of control, so I started this new system where I have a character notebook, a theme notebook, a comedy-writing notebook, a genre notebook, a film-noir notebook, and a thriller notebook. These are three-ring-binder notebooks so I can insert all kinds of material. I collect notes everywhere I go, put them in the file folder, and when I need them, they're there."

One of Sharon's scripts had a supporting character who was a southern transsexual femme fatale named Diane. Diane had a line of dialogue: "In the south we don't call it hot, we call it sultry." I loved the line and asked Sharon how she had come up with it. "It was in one of my file folders of southern dialogue that I overheard. I made a small change, and thought it fit Diane perfectly."

Other writers file their notes on the computer, under many of the same headings.

Most writers take copious notes—and always have notebooks handy. They're prepared to stop and record their words whenever and wherever the Muse comes—in the middle of the freeway, when cooking, eating, bathing, or sleeping.

ORGANIZE

If you haven't already done so, buy file folders and notebooks to start recording what you notice. Use the file folders to organize your story ideas, to file the brilliant dialogue that comes to you at all hours, to store character notes.

As writers, we can't afford to go into automatic pilot. We all need to follow the O.N.E. Principle—Observe. Notice. Experience. In your normal everyday activities, remind yourself to observe and notice what's around you and see its potential for your stories. Constantly write down what you see and hear—potential models for characters, dialogue from the table next to you at the restaurant, the strange incident at the corner. Like artists who sketch anything interesting that they see, the writer sketches details from life.

Robert Rodat (*Saving Private Ryan*) puts snippets of dialogue and character and plot ideas onto 3 x 5 index cards. "I specifically don't put them on a computer, because I want to be able to shuffle them and put them into different orders, so I can see different combinations of ideas."

Most writers move from notes or index card to outlines to writing out the basic events of the story before writing the script. Academy Award-winning writer Ron Bass (*Rain Man*) says, "Before I begin writing a script, I prepare three one-page outlines—one for each act. The outline lists the essential content of the scene and an estimated page count to the nearest half-page per scene. As I begin to write, the story, of course, will change, and when it does, I immediately stop and re-outline."

When Robert Rodat moves to outline, he adds another technique: "When I outline, my office is silent. When I have a clear outline and move to the script, I'll play music appropriate to the scene to set a tonal target and set a mood."

Rodat is not the only writer to set a mood with music. Writer-director Barry Levinson (*Diner*) plays music to match his subject matter. If you use music, consider using music that fits the mood of your story.

Some writers change their visual environment, believing it helps the flow of ideas. Karin Howard (*NeverEnding Story II*) creates a quiet writing mood with candles. Cynthia Whitcomb, who has written more than thirty-five television movies and feature films, decorates her office to match the subject matter of her work. When she was writing an Elvis miniseries, she created an Elvis shrine. "I had Elvis records, an Elvis doll with a guitar, an Elvis telephone that played 'Jailhouse Rock,' and Elvis photos. When I worked on a story about the Senate, I had a Senate hat, mug, mousepad, and notepaper. Now I'm working on a script that takes place in Maine, and I have lobster traps and a rubber lobster named Louis."

Some writers, such as William Nolan (*Burnt Offerings*), write all their drafts by hand.[6]

Carolyn Miller, who writes for the interactive and CD-ROM market (*Toy Story*), uses tons of ugly scratch paper on which she works out her ideas. It keeps her focused on the process, not the results, and she finds it's easier to throw out misguided ideas that are on ugly paper.

Sometimes you need special motivators to write. I have my favorite mugs—the kind of mug I use depends on the mood I'm in. If I have to be very very smart, I'll use my college mug. My cowboy mug makes me brave, when all else fails. My mermaid cup is used for writing about women.

I've also found, under particularly trying writing circumstances, that Hershey bars with almonds are a great boon to the creative process. However, be careful not to make this a daily ritual.

What rituals and props help keep your creative process juiced?

Any ritual that encourages your process and keeps it working can be useful, provided that you don't become too dependent upon the ritual. For some writers, if any part of the ritual breaks down, they can't write.

Writer Karen Croner (*One True Thing*) says, "I used to wake up in the morning and wouldn't speak to anyone before I got to the computer. I believed that it meant everything to write before I spoke. But it was a myth. Ritual can stop you. If ritual gets messed up, then you find you can't write. But a writer writes, no matter what."

Verification

The verification stage verifies and affirms your creative process by helping you evaluate whether you made your script work, got your story right, and created something original. It will also help you determine whether the audience will receive your story with the same passion with which you wrote it. This stage usually begins with your own evaluation of your work, then moves to feedback from friends and consultants, producers and executives, and finally audiences.

You should defer evaluation until you're well into your writing. If you evaluate every word or scene you write as soon as you write it, your critical mind is in control. You can easily become immobilized. You'll be so afraid of making a mistake that you won't write anything at all.

If you ask for outside feedback too soon, when your work is still in its raw, first-draft stage, the verification stage can open up your work to the critical/parental/judgmental voice that tells you, "It's not good enough," and raise your defenses at exactly the time when you want your work to be in flow and in flux. First you brainstorm, then, much later, you evaluate. If you do the two at the same time, you may never write at all.

"I call this the 13th floor of judgment," says script consultant Ingeborg Torgeson. "In the old Russia, the 13th floor of the hotel was reserved for the KGB—the judgmental ones. So, when I write, I imagine getting rid of the 13th floor so those negative voices aren't getting in my way."

In spite of your best intentions, your critical voice may start whining at some point while you're writing. If you can't quiet it by brushing it away, tell it to "Shush!" If that doesn't work, get angry at it. You might try writing out what it's saying and then put your writing in a locked box as if you're muffling a loud gremlin.

You might treat it like a demanding child, and just say, "later." You might tell it, "I don't care how good the writing is, so there!" and thereby diffuse its power. Or you can always tell it, "Linda told me not to listen to you, so go away!" There's room for this critical voice later, but not now.

The verification process will be discussed in the last chapter. Right now, you want to work on the creative flow without any criticism of what is emerging from your process. Let it go. Let it flow. Get to know your Muse. Enjoy her.

3.

Pushing Your Mind to Another Creative Level
· · · · · · · · · · ·

A number of years ago, I had a client who was a leading cancer surgeon. He was highly creative and brilliantly intelligent. His script was set in the future with at least eight subplots and five unique chase scenes and strange people doing strange things. And it made no sense. "I wanted to be imaginative," he said. "Isn't that what creativity is about?"

Yes. But you can't leave your smarts behind.

A few weeks later, a high-level attorney came to my office with a script that was accurate down to the last detail. Beautifully researched. Facts and more facts and more facts. And it was dead on the page. "But isn't screenwriting about telling the truth?" he asked.

Yes. But you can't leave your imagination behind.

You need two kinds of thinking skills to be a great writer. One has already been trained into you in the school system. The other will be expanded through the exercises in this book.

What Are Convergent and Divergent Thinking?

You may have noticed that creative thinking is not highly valued in our culture. School systems reward intelligence, or what's called convergent thinking. Convergent thinking is logical and linear—it moves to the correct answer: "2 + 2 = 4." It rewards accuracy. "The Empire State Building is in the city of New York." It asks for provable facts: How is a trial conducted? What are the usual treatments for cancer? Would an FBI agent or U.S. Marshall chase after a fugitive?

Divergent thinking is flexible thinking—it doesn't approach a problem from a single angle or with the hope of discovering a single answer. It doesn't stick to the old grooves. It doesn't go for the conventional, the staid "we've always done it that way." It considers and plays around with many possibilities.

Divergent thinkers aren't afraid to be silly, ridiculous, crazy, outrageous, and even impossible. Any thought can be useful, and many times you need to go through many ideas before you find the most workable one.

To write great screenplays, you need to employ both convergent and divergent thinking. Convergent thinking is necessary to create well-researched scripts that ring true. Divergent thinking is necessary to make those scripts unique. Screenwriters must know that the Empire State Building is in New York City if they want King Kong to scale it. But they must use divergent thinking when figuring out how to get King Kong from the jungle to the city.

Both forms of thinking are learnable. The more you research to get your facts right, the stronger your convergent thinking skills will become. The more you open your mind to entertain a flood of solutions to any given problem, regardless of their probabilities or logic, the stronger your divergent thinking skills will become.

As you work with the problems posed by the exercises in this book, you may find that some are more difficult than others, and that the solutions may not be readily forthcoming. Don't worry. Just keep practicing. You've been thinking convergently for years. Remember, the creative mind is the child's mind. It loves to discover, explore, and have fun.

YOUR SCRIPT

What in your script needs convergent thinking skills? Where do you use divergent thinking?

Training Divergent Thinking

Divergent thinking emphasizes quantity of ideas in order to find the most original ones. By emphasizing quantity of ideas, it allows the mind to first write down what is obvious and conventional and staid. Then you push your mind past the obvious, forcing yourself to travel a different channel. Throughout this book I ask you to brainstorm an idea—not just to come up with one answer but five or ten or twenty. If you can force yourself to keep thinking, you'll find that your creative mind will be awakened. You'll be surprised at what you start thinking about.

Try employing divergent thinking when writing one of the most often-used scenes in films—the chase scene.

QUESTION

How many different ways can you do a chase scene?

When you begin answering this question, it's very natural for your first five to ten answers to be built on what you remember, what you've seen before, what is obvious.

Here are some scenes that might come to mind:

Car Chase—*The French Connection, Bullitt, Ronin, To Live and Die in L.A.*

Foot chase—*The Fugitive, The Third Man*

Boat chase—James Bond in Venice, the Florida Keys, China.

The boat race in *Face/Off* and *The Killer*

Truck chase—*Smokey and the Bandit, Black Dog*

Horse Race—Most Westerns, plus *Zorro, Butch Cassidy and the Sundance Kid*

BRAINSTORM

Go beyond your initial list and see if you can come up with another ten, twenty, or fifty possibilities. Don't judge. Just write. Be "off the wall."

NOTICE

Somewhere around the tenth or twentieth answer, your mind will start to free up, and you may be surprised at your own originality.

Notice how your mind works.

You might start with vehicles—and move from cars and trucks to a train sidecar, a hot-air balloon, etc. Good. Keep going.

Vehicles might make you think of animal chases. Maybe you have a chase on camels, horses, elephants, giant tortoises, or between giant sloths.

Thinking of animals might make you think of chases in the country—around barns, chasing someone with a hoe, a rake, a hose.

Don't be afraid to let your mind think of the impossible—could you have a chase scene with two people sitting on a rock? Probably not. But since you're not evaluating, write it down. Think impossible thoughts. They might lead you to the possible ones.

You might want to create a diagram that helps you explore chase scenes in a circular rather than a linear model. It might look like this:

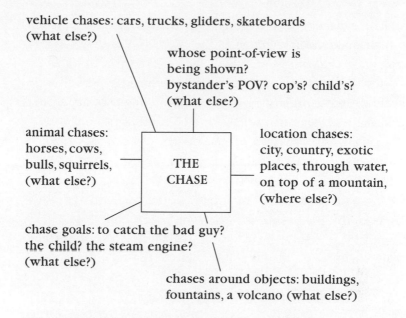

vehicle chases: cars, trucks, gliders, skateboards
(what else?)

whose point-of-view is
being shown?
bystander's POV? cop's? child's?
(what else?)

animal chases:
horses, cows,
bulls, squirrels,
(what else?)

THE
CHASE

location chases:
city, country, exotic
places, through water,
on top of a mountain,
(where else?)

chase goals: to catch the bad guy?
the child? the steam engine?
(what else?)

chases around objects: buildings,
fountains, a volcano (what else?)

Kick-Starting Your Divergent Thinking

No matter how creative you are, sometimes you just get
stuck. You run out of ideas. You can't think of a new approach to the problem. The scene seems dull. The characters stereotyped. The dialogue bland. Working with this
same chase exercise, try some of the following techniques
to see if you come up with new ideas:

ASSOCIATE. When free-associating, you roam from one
idea to another, jumping categories. You might start by asso-
ciating for as long as possible down one category pathway,
and then change to another category. Instead of staying
within the same groove that only thinks of vehicle chases,
you jump to city chases, and that makes you think of sky-
scrapers and tram cars, and that makes you think of the country, which leads you to country music and barnyards and
hoes and other objects to chase with, and that makes your
mind jump to chases in different kinds of weather, which
makes you think of the dry Sahara versus the tropical
rainforest, and that leads you to thinking of *Out of Africa*,

which leads you to imagining a biplane and Robert Redford, which makes you think of chase scenes in *Butch Cassidy and the Sundance Kid*, which then makes you think of bicycles and elephants, which you didn't consider the first time around. Free-associating is a form of circling around, seeing unusual connections, playing one idea off another.

ADD. What could you add to a chase scene to make it more interesting? Addition might include using a car, a truck, and a camel. Addition might mean making it longer or happening in more locations. Come up with ten additions to the ideas you already have.

SUBTRACT. Make it smaller. Shorter. With smaller objects. With smaller people. Take out a part of the chase and see if it becomes more interesting. Come up with ten subtractions to the ideas you've already thought of.

MULTIPLY. Could you have several chases? Instead of two, could you have four? Could you multiply the rabbits in your chase scene? Instead of two cars chasing, could you have four? Come up with ten multiplications to what you've already thought of—no matter how silly.

DIVIDE. Could you have half of a chase scene? Half of a car chasing? Half as many people doing the chasing? Come up with ten divisions to the ideas you already have.

CHANGE YOUR POINT OF VIEW. Could you do the scene from the POV of the bad guy? Or an innocent bystander? Or by having the child chasing the parent? Or the small guy chasing the big guy? What are ten different points of view that would make an interesting chase scene?

DEFINE THE OBJECTIVE. What is the chase scene trying to accomplish? To catch the bad guy? To win a prize? To achieve a dream? By thinking about the objective, you may find that you don't want to catch the bad guy, but to kill him or ensnare him. Or corner him. Or arrest him.

CHANGE THE ACTION. Defining the objective can lead you to questioning the action that the character takes to achieve the goal.

Ask: How many different ways could I catch the bad guy? Setting a trap? Staking out someone's house? Seducing the bad guy into doing something? Putting out bait?

CHANGE THE FUNCTION OF THE ACTION. You might decide that the function of the chase is to catch someone. What if the function were the opposite—to chase someone away? What if the chase looked as if you wanted to catch someone, but it was an illusion? What if a chase were used to throw someone off a trail, rather than follow clues on the trail?

CHANGE THE FUNCTION OF THE PROPS YOU USE. Think of the props that might be part of a chase scene and change their functions. What objects are usually used to chase and catch the bad guy? Your list might include a car, a gun, maybe a phone or a police whistle. Take each of these objects and change its function. You might be chasing with a car. Change the function of the car from a chase vehicle to a road block. You might be thinking of the gun for shooting. Maybe it's used to knock the guy out. You might be thinking of the police whistle to alert others. Maybe it's used instead to gag the guy and keep him quiet.

Now think of objects that could be used to get the bad guy. What if their usual functions were changed? How might the following objects be used to catch someone? A hoe? A fishing net? A steering wheel? A dumpster?

You might also get some creative juice out of thinking how a chase scene would be done if MacGyver were using unusual objects to stop someone.

ASK "WHY?" This is one of the best ways to awaken the creative mind. Asking "Why?" takes you out of the groove that says, "It has to be this way" and opens up your mind to all possibilities. Why does it have to be a good guy chasing a bad guy? Why does it have to be a guy at all? Why do they have to do it in the United States? Why does the chase have to be in the third act?

Ask "Why?" of all the previous creative techniques. Why do I need to add or subtract? Could I do them both? Why would I need to do any of these techniques? What would happen if I did something else instead? What if I just went with my original idea? Why does it have to be a chase scene?

You can use this same collection of techniques with love scenes, danger scenes, getting-to-know-you scenes, and climbing-the-corporate-ladder scenes.

YOUR SCRIPT

Look at an action you use in your script. Using each of these techniques, see if you can make it more unique, more creative, different.

Throughout this book, when you run out of ideas, go through the stages of the creative process: Remember your own experience. Prepare and Research. Define the problem. Incubate the idea. Prod the Muse to come up with solutions. Go back to these creative techniques. Associate. Add. Subtract. Multiply. Divide. Change your Point of View. Define the Objective. Change the Function. Ask "Why?"

4.

Enriching and Refining Your Storytelling Skills

Good screenwriters write about anything—their first love, the perfect murder, what might happen when the Martians come.

Great screenwriters also write about anything. But there's a difference. Great writers know how to rev up a story and make it in to a dynamo. They know how to twist it and turn it. They make it seem special, different, grounded in experience. They give it shocking and surprising details that make you realize it could only be built on the uniqueness of truth.

You've probably experienced the problems that writing down a story can cause. Stories can have trouble finding their shape. And if you don't know how to shape a story, you don't know how a tell a story. Audiences come to the theater to see a story well told. They want a narrative, not episodes. They want the story to feel of one piece, rather than a lot of interesting but disjointed scenes.

The screenwriter's work is to find great stories and shape these stories into dramatic form.

Dramatic, well-crafted stories have clearly defined, carefully considered beginnings, middles, and ends. Yet, most of the time, stories come to us in pieces. We might have the ending (he was arrested) and know the beginning (there was a murder), but we might not know much about the middle. We might not know who investigated, how difficult the investigation was, whether there were conflicts between detectives, whether there was danger, whether there were late nights that led to conflicts with the family, whether the detectives are sure they got the right guy.

Or you might know the middle (there was a riot) but not know how it started or how it was resolved.

In this chapter, we want to look at the *practice* of good storytelling and use imagination to make up stories and add scenes where scenes are missing. As a screenwriter, you want to get the feel for a story into your head, your imagination, your whole being.

As you work with the following stories or parts of stories, think of them in terms of a beginning (Act One), a middle (Act Two), and an end (Act Three). Between each act are turning points, which twist and turn the action. Sometimes a turning point shows a character making a decision. It changes the focus of the story so the next act is about a different kind of action than the act before.[1]

Working With Your Favorite Films

THINK

Think of one of your favorite movies, and tell the story as clearly as possible in two to five minutes. Do this exercise with at least ten films.

The easiest stories to tell are usually mystery stories and detective stories. They generally have a clear catalyst and first-act action (a crime is committed, a detective is assigned to the case), a clear second-act action (an investigation), and a clear third act, leading to a climax (the shoot-'em-up or chase, leading to the capture or destruction of the bad guy). That's why every year you'll see hundreds of scripts written for television cop shows and feature films about the cop going after the bad guy.

Of course, great detective stories find ways to make the conventional seem complex and imaginative. Look at *L.A. Confidential* or *Silence of the Lambs* to see the variety and complexity that can come from following a classic structure while using twists, turns, and rich character details.

> Tell the story of some classic detective or mystery films, such as *Dial M for Murder, Sorry, Wrong Number, Witness, Psycho, Body Heat, The Firm, Double Indemnity, Rear Window, The Big Sleep, The Maltese Falcon, Rebecca,* and *The Silence of the Lambs.* What other detective stories come to mind?

Underdog triumph stories are also fairly easy to tell. In Act One, the underdog is introduced along with a contest or goal. Act Two shows practice and rehearsal. Act Three focuses on the final competition.

> Tell the story of such classic underdog triumph stories as *Rocky, The Karate Kid, Dirty Dancing, Footloose, Good Will Hunting, The Truman Show, My Left Foot, The Color Purple, Forrest Gump, Norma Rae, Amistad, Breaking Away, Rudy,* and *The Bad News Bears.*

Romantic comedies are usually structured with a clear beginning, middle, and end—they meet, they get to know each other, they get together.

Tell the stories of such romantic comedies as *My Best Friend's Wedding, As Good as It Gets, When Harry Met Sally, It Happened One Night, Sabrina, Ghost, Four Weddings and a Funeral,* and *Sleepless in Seattle.*

As you tell the story, do you notice how different each film can be, even though its structure might be similar to that of many other films?

Whenever you go to a film, re-tell that film's story in terms of its beginning, middle, and end. Learn to tell it as if it were a one-minute pitch. This will hone your skills at recognizing story structure, while also preparing you for pitch meetings when you may only have one minute to give a fast but concise overview of a story.

If you spend just one hour practicing this exercise on a variety of films, you'll be amazed at how well it will pay off in all your future stories.

EXAMPLE OF THE ONE-MINUTE PITCH: THE FUGITIVE

There's a murder. It's the wife of successful vascular surgeon—Dr. Richard Kimble. All evidence points to him, but he knows a one-armed man did it. Kimble is arrested, convicted, and sentenced to death. On the road to the prison, there's a fight in the bus. The bus crashes on the railroad tracks and is hit by a train. Kimble escapes. Immediately, U.S. Marshall Sam Gerard is put on the case. He's the guy who always gets his man—fast. But Kimble is a worthy adversary. A cat-and-mouse chase follows as Kimble tries to try to find the one-armed man and Gerard follows clues and Kimble sightings. Kimble finds the one-armed man, but realizes he's not the brains behind the murder. All evidence soon points to his best friend—Dr. Charlie Nichols. As he goes to confront Charlie, Gerard also begins to suspect Kimble is innocent. Gerard follows Kimble—and all meet in a three-way fight between Nichols, Kimble, and Gerard, which results in Gerard realizing that Kimble is an innocent man. Kimble is freed.

YOUR SCRIPT

Work on a one-minute pitch about your story. Is it clear? Does it have a beginning, a middle, and an end?

Make a list of your favorite films, whether simple or complex. Tell their stories. Do they all have clear beginnings, middles, and ends?

REFLECT

As you analyze a film, notice if there's some place where you get stuck in its story. This tells you that some event didn't connect with other parts of the story. Are there any places where you ask, "Why? What happened? How did they get from here to there? Did I miss something?"

Sometimes, you'll notice that when you tell the story after you see the film, you get confused. If so, go back and see the film again. Did the writer skip some important event that was necessary to make the story make sense, or are you having difficulty remembering because it's a complex story? A complex film can work well when viewing it, but you might need additional viewings in order to remember all its details. *L.A. Confidential* is one of these films, as is *Dangerous Liaisons*. I'm fascinated by both of these films, but they take some study to be able to track all their storylines and plot intricacies.

Sometimes, after viewing a film, you start discussing the subplots or relationship stories, rather than the main plotline, which is usually the action story (or A story). If so, this might indicate that the balance between plots and subplots is not working. Or maybe you weren't focused on the driving A story, which pushes the story from the beginning through the middle to the end.

For instance, if you were telling the story of *Shakespeare in Love*, you would certainly discuss the subplot of the love between Will and Viola. But if you forgot to mention that Shakespeare had to write a play in a short amount of time and was desperate for a Muse to inspire him, you would have missed the action story of the film. When telling a story, you want to be aware of the integration of both these storylines—the action story and the relationship story (or stories, since films often have more than one relational subplot story).

As you analyze films, notice the problem areas that can be found in even award-winning or commercially successful films. Some films flash with brilliance but fall apart in certain sections—usually the second half of Act Two. One of my favorite films is *Seven Brides for Seven Brothers*. When I analyze it, it's clear to me that it has a great beginning and middle, but the last half of Act Two begins to drag and Act Three isn't quite long enough to really build the suspense. I still love the film, but I'd be one of the first to say, "It's not perfect."

I love *Cinema Paradiso*, but the first five minutes seem unfocused, the last half of Act Two drags (when Toto stands underneath his beloved's window, then goes into the army), and Act Three is too long.

Don't be afraid to critique great films as well as good ones. You can respect a film while still noticing that something is missing.

YOUR SCRIPT

Is there any place where your story seems muddled or out of balance?

Write From Your Personal Stories

Everyone has hundreds of stories in his/her background. These can be the start of an unforgettable film. You have the stories you've experienced, but also the stories that you've been told about complex lives, strange decisions, and conflicts of years ago that may have changed your life.

COLLECT

Start collecting true-life stories. Place them in a file folder, loose-leaf notebook, or accordion folder. Talk to friends, relatives, colleagues. Label the stories for future reference. You might use such labels as "period pieces," "love stories," "mysteries," "family dramas," etc.

One of my favorite stories is about my great-great-grandmother Henrietta, from Hanover, Germany. She was married to an engineer who was hired by the Czar to build bridges in Russia. He left her and their four children, built the bridges, and returned home four years later with Russian jewels and a woman he called "the maid." The maid was lovely and young and just happened to have a three-year-old son who looked remarkably like the husband. Now Henrietta was no pushover. Recognizing the situation, she gathered her four children together, and of course the jewels, and announced to her husband, "I'm going to America and you will never see your children again!" Henrietta came to the U.S. and got rich by starting a cookie company that was eventually bought out by Nestlé's. The five garnets that she passed on to my grandmother are now in the hands of my niece.

Although this is only a broad narrative, I'm fascinated by this gutsy woman. By putting the paragraph in a file folder, I've preserved it and made it accessible for my use at some later date.

THINK

What stories from your own life interest you?

There might have been a romance that changed your life (*Summer of '42, Before Sunrise, When Harry Met Sally*). Or a trip you took (*City Slickers, Trip to Bountiful*).

Perhaps you competed in a contest or overcame some obstacle or challenge (*Rocky, Karate Kid, Shine, The Other Side of the Mountain, Chariots of Fire*).

Maybe you met a teacher who changed your life (*Educating Rita, Dead Poets Society, To Sir with Love, Stand and Deliver*).

WRITE

Write out your stories as synopses. Even if you only have snippets of a story, jot down what you remember.

ANALYZE

After you have thirty or forty ideas, see if they have common themes, common locations, common character types, common genres, or common values. Finding commonalities will tell you which stories engage you and intrigue you and speak to you. This process will help lead you to your own personal voice.

Look at each story. Does each one have a beginning, a middle, an end? If not, create the missing pieces.

YOUR SCRIPT

Does any part of your script come from a personal experience or a story you were told? Have you had personal experiences that you can draw upon to deepen your story? To make your story more authentic?

Begin With the Beginning

In the following exercises, you're going to start writing stories, working around a central event and making up the rest. Many stories are created in a linear fashion—you start with a catalyst and build your story through a cause-and-effect process. This model works like dominoes. The catalyst is the toppling of the first domino, which then topples the next, and the next, and the next...until the last domino falls at the end of the film.

Other stories are created in a circular fashion. You might begin with ideas for the end or the middle, not even being sure about what starts your story or where it's going. You circle around your story, looking at it from different angles, gradually seeing a pattern emerging.

Or maybe you start with the perimeter, as if you're constructing a puzzle. You see a frame, maybe even knowing the beginning and the end but not the middle. Gradually, you fill it in, section by section, eventually doubling back to pick up any missing pieces.

For these types of stories, your work process might involve making notes on index cards or scratch paper or in a journal or narrating ideas into a tape recorder. From these materials—snippets of ideas to fully written scenes—you can then create outlines or treatments that synopsize your story or write the full script.

You can do the following exercises a number of times, working with my story or with your own, challenging yourself to come up with five or ten different possibilities, then changing genres to consider other alternatives. Just as I've looked at my own life to find dramatic possibilities, do the same with your own personal stories.

The Story Beginning

Several years ago, I was with a friend in Berlin. As we stood on a street corner waiting for the light to change, my friend, Dulcie, suddenly grabbed my shoulder and pulled me aside.As I turned around to see what was happening, fleeting thoughts came to me—was someone trying to attack me? to stab me? I turned around and saw an elderly man with his arm out as if to put it on my shoulder.When Dulcie pulled me out of his way, he lost his balance and fell, hard, on the pavement. Dulcie and I immediately realized he was drunk and had tried to put his arm on my shoulder to steady himself.As we moved to help him, I saw his head was bleeding. Suddenly a car came around the corner and ran over his glasses, which had fallen into the street. Dulcie, who spoke German, immediately went for help while I stayed with him. Others gathered around, some putting a sweater under his head, others just watching. I wondered if he would die in front of me but remembered that my husband (who's in the medical profession) had once told me that head wounds bleed a great deal, but aren't necessarily as bad as they seem. He also told me to watch a person's eyes. If they don't glaze over, he'll probably be all right.When I felt reasonably sure he'd live, my more dramatic side kicked in. I figured that, in circumstances such as this, the guy needs a pretty face to look at and a hand to hold. I looked around—no pretty faces to be seen. (Most of the people around me were un-pretty men.) Dulcie, who had a particularly pretty face, was nowhere to be seen. I figured I was the closest he'd get, so I knelt down next to him and took his hand. Soon the ambulance came.

This could make a good beginning for a film. But if you started writing this beginning, where would it go from here?

Define the problem that you're trying to solve.You might phrase it as: "I have to find some ongoing connection with this man to get the story to develop.There will need to be some mystery, some intrigue, something that will get my character unwittingly involved."

You might start by looking for something that pulls your character into the story. Might he have given me something surreptitiously that I must deliver somewhere? To whom might I need to deliver it? Might he have been stabbed or shot? (See the beginning of Alfred Hitchcock's *The Man Who Knew Too Much*.) If I talked to him, might I then be followed after he got into an ambulance? If he were killed, what kind of character would I need to be to follow up some clues? A detective? A journalist? A crazy tourist who loves mysteries? What if he had lived? What if he were younger?

What are the possible subplots in this story? A relationship with the man? With my friend Dulcie? With the job I was doing that brought me to Berlin?

Now think through possible genres. What if this story were a political intrigue? A mystery? A detective story? A comedy? A romance?

If you are doing these exercises in a group, each of you might work out a story for your next meeting. You might also brainstorm together in the group.

YOUR SCRIPT

Which of your personal stories would make a good catalyst for a film?

Start With Your Own Turning Points

The First Turning Point

You could start creating a story by working with the first turning point, which would lead you into Act Two. As you read my following story, see if you can think of first turning points in your own life.

Monday. I was teaching for RAI Television in Rome. Ahead of me lay a three-week schedule that included teaching in Berlin, Copenhagen, and London, book-signings and television appearances to promote *When Women Call the Shots*, and having a grand time on my longest European tour. An elderly Italian gentleman had just approached me while I was having breakfast and told me I was more beautiful than Rome. All was going well. Life was good. Monday afternoon I received a phone call. My dear friend Cathleen had just been diagnosed with breast cancer. Her operation would be Friday. Her ten-year-old son is my godson, and I felt love and responsibility to her and to her son. I was also immediately aware of my responsibility to the people who had planned my European seminars for the last six months, including the woman in London who had invested thousands of dollars of her own money to promote my seminar. Should I stay or go?

Imagine how the second act of my story would evolve. If I stayed to continue my teaching, Cathleen would be a subplot in my teaching-adventure main plot. I would keep the subplot alive through telephone calls and faxes. If I left, my main story would become a disease story, rather than an adventure story. However, there might be professional repercussions that could become the subplot.

What did I do? I returned home. Being with Cathleen through her illness was one of the richest experiences of my life. The subplot overseas continued—I asked my colleague Dara Marks if she would leave for Europe within the week to teach my classes. Another subplot developed as well—a deeper relationship with my godson.

REFLECT

Which of your personal stories contains a good first turning point? Have you ever made a decision such as this? What changes would you make to create a strong dramatic script?

The Second Turning Point

Here's a second turning point and a third act from my life. See if you can fill in a possible beginning, middle, and end.

I was about twenty-six years old. It was summer. I was teaching drama at a camp in northern California. On my day off, Gail (another employee) and I decided that we'd go for a hike to Seven Falls. Gail was an outdoorswoman—so I suggested she lead the way. As we proceeded on our hike, I noticed that the trail Gail had chosen was getting narrower and narrower. Soon, we were walking along a small ledge. I told Gail, "This looks dangerous. There has to be a better way!" "No, it's fine," she answered as she worked her way down from one ledge to another. As I tried to follow, I realized I couldn't get down without holding on to something. I saw a small bush rooted in the rock. I held on to it, carefully trying to move onto the ledge where Gail waited. She held out her hand. Should I trust Gail or the bush? I decided to trust Gail. As I gave her my hand, the bush uprooted. My feet started to slip over the cliff. "Dig in, dig in!" Gail yelled. I slammed my feet into the side of the hill, and stopped my fall. We looked around. There was no other place to go. I looked up. There was a huge slippery moss-covered boulder that clearly could not be traversed. I looked down. There was a steep rock, with a very small ledge below it and then a long way down a steep hill. I was sure that we couldn't slide down the rock without falling down the hill. I looked back—we had destroyed our way out—the bush was no longer there.

Gail decided that we'd slide down the rock to the ledge. Since I didn't believe it was possible, I asked her to go first and to catch me. She started sliding down the rock. But she didn't stop. She rolled and rolled and rolled, finally out of sight. All was quiet. I yelled to her. There was no answer. Was she hurt? Dead?

How would I get down, knowing that the only way down was the way Gail had gone? Could I do it without falling off the mountain?

How do you think this got resolved? Was I rescued by a ranger? Was Gail all right? Could she come up and help me? If she were hurt, how would I get her out of there? What if she were dead? Would the camp send out a search party because we didn't come back in time? Might it soon be dark? Might it rain or snow? What's the ending for the Linda and Gail Adventure?

I noticed a tree to the left of the ledge and figured that if I could roll down the boulder at an angle, I could stop my fall by rolling into it. It worked. I managed to get down the hill. Gail had hurt her knee and her ankle, although she could still walk with some help. I knew I had to get her out of there before dark. We were helped out of the wilderness by a naked man who was camping nearby (honest! although he went to get some clothes). We got back to the camp in time. And I ended up dating the guy who helped us.

If you were working with the man as a subplot, you might think it would make a good romantic subplot. But, he'd need to be introduced earlier, since you wouldn't wait to introduce a subplot in your last act. In actuality, his appearance did not begin in the third act. He used to work at the camp where I was working. Although I had never met him, Gail had. So when he came over to help Gail, she recognized him. If this were a drama with a subplot, I would have needed to meet him at an earlier point. This meeting could have resulted in friendship interest or some tension between us, so that the second turning point of the adventure story would also be a second turning point in the romantic subplot. It was already there in the real-life story. It just needed to be pulled out and re-shaped.

CREATE

Remembering that one of the elements of creativity is the ability to combine unlike elements, see if you can think of a way to combine my three stories into one story. Of course, there are no rules for doing this. You can change any elements to make them fit together.

YOUR SCRIPT

Is there any part of your script that's based on a choice or crisis from your own life? Write about it. Does it add any further insight or nuance to the script?

Breaking Down Stories You've Collected

Although some writers only have one or two good ideas and may spend several years working out one of them, many writers are overflowing with stories. They're constantly on the lookout for them. They find them. They remember them. They collect them.

As a writer, you want to be an idea-collector, a story-gatherer. You can begin anywhere and collect anything that looks interesting. You become like a crow, choosing any shiny bauble for the nest, not knowing what will be the most usable. Look in likely—as well as unlikely—places. You might start with newspapers, where you can find plenty of crime stories, human dramas, and political intrigue. Don't forget the tabloids, which have great ideas for science-fiction stories ("Woman gives birth to rabbit by eating too many carrots") or introduces you to bizarre behavior and strange events ("Elvis seen skiing in Hawaii").

Then spread your creative net further afield. Check out *People, Rolling Stone, Reader's Digest, Mother Jones, The New Yorker*. Don't forget ham radio, the local news, the Internet, and the foreign press.

If you look at newspaper clippings, you'll see many reporters focus on story beginnings and story endings. Sometimes the event they report could be either one. Someone got a promotion. If this event were a beginning, it might look like *Tootsie* or *Wall Street* or *Big*. If it were an ending, the movie might look like *Working Girl* or *9 to 5* or *Jerry Maguire*.

Other newspaper stories might tell of a murder—the beginning event that starts an investigation.

Or there might have been a revolution or a riot—which starts a war.

On Tuesday, October 6, 1998, I read the *International Herald Tribune* at the airport in Stockholm. Here are the stories I found. As you read each of them, think about whether it's a beginning, a middle, or an end, and what genre might best express the story.

(1) The lead article was about the impeachment inquiry against Clinton. Here was a story with a clear beginning (the trysts with Monica and the Linda Tripp tapes), a good first turning point (the news breaks), a strong second act (more details come out, leading to the grand jury). The second turning point is the beginning of the impeachment inquiry. The Third Act is the trial in the House and Senate, and The Climax is the acquittal.

What's the genre? Political drama? Comedy? Tragedy? All three?

(2) A pilot who was part of a team that bombed a dam during World War II died. This "brazen British bombing carried out with high-spirited élan" was a crucial strike during World War II.

Would this be the beginning of your story or the end? Would this be a war movie? An action-adventure? A comedy? A caper film?

(3) An oil pipeline in Turkmenastin is being fought over by Moscow, Washington, and Iraq. The fight has stopped oil production, and led each country to figure out how, underhandedly, they can route the oil out of Turkmenistan without the other countries realizing it.

What part of the story structure do you have here? What genre might you use? Political comedy? Political drama?

(4) Chun Callen has resided at St. Elizabeth's psychiatric hospital since 1989, when she committed an irrational

act—she came to the White House to talk to the president about her divorce.

Where would you use this information in a script? To start a story? Would you create a journalist story? A hospital corruption story? A government corruption story? A political comedy? Might you use it as a subplot?

(5) The top Japanese-born Sumo wrestler, who is 6 foot 8 and 516 pounds, just married a schoolteacher. He was dressed in the traditional wedding attire of a golden hahakam skirt and a white-crested kimono.

How would the story change if the wedding were the end of the story? If it were the beginning of the story? Would you make this a romantic comedy? A farce? A musical comedy (à la *The King and I*)?

Do this same exercise by taking storylines from the tabloids.[2]

This is an exercise that you can do daily, quickly skimming the newspaper to collect possibilities.

Creating Stories Through Snippets of Information

Sometimes you have an idea that carries with it very little information, but something about the idea intrigues you. All you have is a very small idea, an image, a character description, a situation.

CREATE

Create a well-structured story for each of these situations:

1. Johnny-O is returning from Las Vegas on Pioneer Airlines after getting his fifth quickie divorce. But this one was different. Boy, was it different.

2. She was intricately and delicately dismantling the bomb when she noticed something. This could only have been the work of one person.

3. Considering the circumstances, there was only one thing for her to do—she'd have to hide out in Tibet.

CREATE

Take each of these situations and come up with five different storylines.

Change genres, and see what other kinds of stories evolve.

Change supporting characters, and see how that would change the story.

Take each situation, change at least one word in it, and see what new ideas emerge. For instance, instead of the fifth quickie divorce, maybe it was his fifth quickie murder. Instead of a bomb, she's dismantling a vase. Instead of hiding out in Tibet, she has to marry him in Tibet.

Challenge yourself to be ridiculous. See if you get creative flashes by changing several words and inserting words that make your brain pop with a giggle or a shock of possibilities. What else might she do in Tibet? Steal Tibet? Garden Tibet? Invade Tibet? Introduce green elephants to Tibet? What if it weren't Tibet? What kind of ideas would you get if it were Ecuador? Ghana? Sandusky, Ohio?

Affirm Your Strengths, Develop Your Weaknesses

By now, some of you may have found the exercises fun and easy. Others may have found them challenging and had difficulty identifying the structural elements. If so, consider two possibilities. If some of these exercises were difficult, you've found out something very important about yourself—structure does not come naturally to you. If you are not a structuralist, you might decide to move ahead to the chapters on character, theme, or becoming a sensation-thinker to attempt to identify your strong points. Then, once you're assured that you have some (and I can guarantee that you do!), you can use those chapters to affirm your own individual process, and then, with that confidence, return to this chapter to work again on the exercises.

Or you might decide to do a story exercise every day— work on it, digest the information, and keep using it until it feels natural.

5.

Exploring Your Themes
and Ideas

What does your script mean? What's it about? Does your script engage the mind, making it snap to attention?

Great writers have something to say and they know how to say it. They have ideas that get under your skin. Ideas that prick at you, grab at you, and don't let go. Sometimes these ideas come flooding back at you, years later. They clarify the meaning of our human experience. They give a film substance.

Unfortunately, some writers with good ideas don't flesh out their themes. They discuss them. They sermonize—rather than humanize—their themes.

Themes can seem abstract and amorphous. But themes are the meaning we bring to the issues and problems we face in life. We try to make sense out of our experiences. We try to see them from a larger perspective. We try to learn from them, so we don't repeat the same mistakes again.

Why are you writing your particular story? Maybe because you have a perspective you want to communicate about this particular experience. It might be as simple as the idea that you believe that good can triumph against bad. Or that we can defeat the monster, no matter how in-vulnerable he seems. And you prove your theme through the ending of your story. The happy ending shows that you believe that all can turn out well. The cynical ending shows another perspective about the frustration and lack of reso-lution in life.

In our daily life, we live out different themes. Sometimes we're greedy or seek fame or chase after money and power. Sometimes our themes are about winning the race or get-ting the prettiest gal or the handsomest guy. Sometimes we're fish out of water, feeling uncertain on unfamiliar ground. Sometimes we're the big fish in the little pond or the little fish in the big pond. Sometimes we're the out-sider. We feel like the alien who's out of sorts with the rest of the world.

We grow physically, which brings up themes about how we look, how we feel about ourselves—self-perception and self-esteem. Even the gorgeous hunks and the beautiful babes have personal and physical issues to resolve.

Our desire for self-fulfillment presents such issues as finding ourselves, coming of age, fulfilling our calling, and using our talents.

Through your theme, you have an opportunity to present your philosophy of life, your value system, your world view. It's your chance to share your ideas about life, provided you don't preach about it, but share it through the medium of story, characters, and cinematic images.

Some writers begin their scripts with ideas they want to explore. Perhaps you want to explore what you learned from a failed romance and believe an audience might ben-efit from your hard-won insight. At first, this idea may be no more than an inkling. But then you start to pursue it. What story will express it best? What characters will em-body it? What images will best convey its subtleties? In this fashion, you work your way around the theme, which, during the course of your work, may change. By the time you finish your script, it may no longer be about failed romance but about being open to new love.

Some writers let their themes emerge through the writing, allowing their unconscious to lead them, even when they're not sure what they want to say, or why they're saying it. They explain that their themes never become clear until they've finished writing the script. Then they rewrite, strengthening and clarifying the theme.

Many of the same themes have been used over and over again in some of our most successful films, but always with a different slant, depending on the writer.

BRAINSTORM

Look at the following list. How many films can you think of that explore these ideas?

THE UNDERDOG TRIUMPHS—*Rocky*, *The Verdict*, *Norma Rae*

FISH OUT OF WATER—*Nell*, *Forrest Gump*, *E.T.*

STRANGER IN A STRANGE LAND—*Local Hero*, *Witness*, *Edward Scissorhands*

COMMUNITY—*Eve's Bayou*, *Grand Canyon*, *How to Make an American Quilt*

INTEGRITY—*To Kill a Mockingbird*, *Mr. Holland's Opus*

OVERCOMING ADVERSITY—*Shine*, *My Left Foot*, *Mask*

SURVIVAL OF THE FITTEST—*Mad Max*, *The Road Warrior*

POWER AND CONTROL—*Apocalypse Now*, *Silence of the Lambs*

MANIPULATION—*Blade Runner*, *Working Girl*

GREED—*Wall Street*, *Goldfinger*

BETRAYAL—*Betrayed*, *Fatal Attraction*

CORRUPTION—*L.A. Confidential*, *Quiz Show*, *Chinatown*

JUSTICE AND/OR INJUSTICE—*The Fugitive*, *A Civil Action*

INNOCENCE—*Forrest Gump*, *The Secret of Roan Inish*, *Being There*

IDENTITY—*Sixteen Candles, The Breakfast Club, Stand by Me*
CREATIVITY AND CONFORMITY—*Dead Poets Society, Bagdad Cafe, Theo and Vincent*
FINDING LOVE—*Moonstruck, The English Patient*
CLASSISM—*Wuthering Heights*
SEXISM—*Disclosure*
RACISM—*Mississippi Masala, Mississipi Burning, To Kill a Mockingbird*

THINK

What have these films taught you about these issues?
How have their writers shown the themes?

As you analyze and explore the themes of these films, notice that the themes are active, not static. They develop throughout the script. A character finds identity. Characters overcome racism or sexism or classism. They find love. Triumph. Conquer. Grow from innocence to wisdom. Overcome corruption. Show that Greed is not the highest value. Creativity wins out over conformity. And strangers in a strange land either find community and connection or realize that there's no place like home.

You can map out a film's thematic movement by looking at where the central character begins in the story and where he or she ends up. Does the character undergo a transformation? What are the steps in this transformational journey?

YOUR SCRIPT

Does your script contain any of the themes listed above? If so, analyze the films associated with those themes, studying the ways they've been worked with before.

How Does the Writer Communicate Theme?

When different writers utilize the same theme, each writer's personal understanding of the issue will present a unique point of view.

For instance, in the mid-1980s, three very different films explored COMMUNITY. *Places in the Heart* taught us that community is more than our nuclear family and that the bonds of love can include the outsider. *Witness* showed the clash of cultures between two very different communities—the non-violent Amish and a small group of violent and corrupt policemen. *Police Academy II* showed us, in a farcical manner, the collaboration that is essential if a community (the police) is to overcome evil and keep the bad guys at bay. Although this last example is mindless, even idiotic, it shows that commercially successful films, no matter what their genre, still contain an underlying idea.

REFLECT

What do you learn about LOVE AND MARRIAGE when you watch That Old Feeling or My Best Friend's Wedding or When Harry Met Sally or Sleepless in Seattle?

What insights do you gain about transformation by watching The Graduate or Unforgiven?

What do you learn about SUCCESS and ACHIEVE-MENT by watching Wall Street or Goodfellas or You've Got Mail?

Great writers communicate theme through action and images, with good dialogue used sparingly. They prove their theme by showing it, not talking about it.

Themes in screenwriting can be tricky because in real-life we love to talk about our themes—share our

philosophies of life, tell people our beliefs about life's meaning. But the themes we talk about are not our life's real
themes. Our true themes are lived out by our actions. The
character is the theme. Truth is what we see, not what we're
told.

ANALYZE

To begin to get theme into your mind and fingertips,
choose one of the themes from my list above, and
choose a film that communicates that theme.

How did the writer communicate the theme in this
film? Did the writer use dialogue? Action? Images?
List the thematic moments that you remember
from the film.

Sometimes themes are communicated through dialogue.
If used in dialogue, the theme needs to be expressed
quickly and succinctly, usually in one or two lines. In *Wall
Street*, Gordon Gekko says the theme a number of times:

> GORDON GEKKO
> Greed is good.
>
> What's worth doing is worth doing for money...
>
> It's all about bucks...
>
> You're going to parachute out a rich man.

His thematic statements are contrasted with the voices of
integrity—Carl and Lou.

> LOU
> Remember, there are no shortcuts...
>
> The main thing about money, it makes you do
> things you don't want to...

A man looks into the abyss. There's nothing star-
ing back at him. At that moment man finds his
character. And that's what keeps him out of the
abyss.

CARL
Never measure a man's success by the size of his
wallet.

Each of these thematic statements is proven in the film.
We see Bud (Charlie Sheen) doing things he doesn't want
to. We see him trying to take shortcuts. We see him looking
into the abyss and finding his character. We see him trying
to measure Gekko's success by the size of his wallet. And
we see him learning that his father is the only honest man
he knows.

The film *Room with a View* is about identity and finding meaning.

MR. EMERSON
(to Lucy Honeychurch)
I don't require you to fall in love with my boy, but
if anyone could keep him from brooding . . .
please make my boy realize that at the side of the
everlasting Why, there is a Yes and a Yes and a Yes.

Lucy, who is not known for her philosophical mindset, tries
to figure out a way to help:

LUCY HONEYCHURCH
Has your son a particular hobby?

And George Emerson discovers the yes when he falls in
love with Lucy.

The film *Schindler's List* says the theme when the one-
armed man tells Schindler:

THE ONE-ARMED MAN
(to Oskar Schindler)
You are a good man.

It repeats the theme when Oskar Schindler asks Itzhak
Stern to draw up a list of all the people he'll relocate to
save them from the death camps.

STERN
This list is an absolute good. The list is life—all
around its margins...

And the film proves that this is true.

ANALYZE

Watch films and listen for their thematic statements. Some films with clear, well-integrated thematic statements include *Contact, The Wizard of
Oz, A Civil Action, The People vs. Larry Flynt, Les
Misérables, Enemy of the State, A Few Good Men,*
etc.

Sometimes films illustrate their themes by showing different characters representing different thematic aspects.
In *Dead Poets Society*, each character expands the theme
of creativity vs. conformity. Keating shows us that creativity is the spice and joy of life. Mr. Nolan represents the fear
some feel when someone creative messes up the way he's
always done things. Todd shows that creativity can help
one find his/her identity. Charlie shows creativity out of
control. Knox shows that creativity can be used to "woo
women." And Neil shows that creativity demands an inner
strength to stand up to conformity or it can lead to death.

One Flew Over The Cuckoo's Nest shows each character representing a different aspect of the theme of tyranny
vs. liberation. McMurphy represents liberation and Nurse

Ratched represents tyranny. Various other characters represent what our society tyrannizes—the Indian, the homosexual, the weakling, the mama's boy. McMurphy liberates them, helping them discover their identities.

In *Sense and Sensibility*, we learn about the different faces of love through the variety of characters. Some characters express impetuous love. Others represent sensible love, sacrificial love, love betrayed, appropriate love, and conventional love.

WRITE

Write out the thematic scenes as you remember them in any of these above-mentioned films. Try to capture the characters, the dialogue, the images of the scenes. If you're not sure how a scene worked thematically, watch the film again and copy the dialogue as you watch it. After you write out several scenes, the difference between those writers who clearly communicate their themes and those writers who make them a muddle should be clearer.

Although copying is not considered a viable creative act, it can be part of a learning process. Picasso said that he copied other people's work when he was learning so that he didn't have to copy it later on.

CREATE

Imagine that you've been hired to rewrite a script because the producer wants its themes to be stronger. Create two new thematic scenes. If possible, don't use dialogue to communicate the theme—use images and character actions.

REFLECT

What films best express your philosophy and point-of-view?

YOUR SCRIPT

How does your work communicate your theme? How much of it is communicated through dialogue? If a deaf person were watching your film, would s/he understand the ideas you're trying to communicate?

Finding Your Thematic Voice

Part of your job as a writer is to help audiences make sense of their own personal experiences. Characters act out a complete story-with-theme-and-consequences right before our eyes. During the film, we identify with the characters, follow their journey, and gain insight to apply to our own lives.

Insights may be negative: "Crime doesn't pay." Insights may be positive: "Dreams can come true." Whether they are positive or negative, themes differentiate one person's life from another's. While some people live out themes of suffering and abusing themselves or those around them, others live out themes of triumphing over adversity and creating a better world.

Our themes change as our life situations change. If you're in the act of selling a script, you might embody such themes as ambition and perseverance. But if you just stumbled onto a big-name producer who wants to produce your first script, you might embody themes of luck and wish-fulfillment.

What is your personal life philosophy?
Do you believe you can do anything?
That truth will triumph? That justice prevails?
That good pays off? That love endures?

What experiences and influential people led you to this philosophy?

Working With Your Personal Themes

In the previous exercises, you began with someone else's film, and used convergent (analytical) thinking to figure out how the writer worked with theme. In the next set of exercises, you're going to reverse the process, using divergent (imaginative) thinking to create themes out of your own experiences.

REFLECT

List some of the issues you've confronted in your life.

Your list might include such major life reversals or transformations as:
DIVORCE
FINDING LOVE
MARRIAGE
UNEMPLOYMENT
FINDING FRIENDS AND OVERCOMING ISOLATION
HAVING CHILDREN
WANTED OR UNWANTED PREGNANCY
AN UNCERTAIN FUTURE
GRADUATION OR PROMOTION AND OTHER LIFE TRANSITIONS
FINDING FULFILLMENT
FINDING YOUR IDENTITY
FIGHTING AGAINST CONFORMITY
LOSING INTEGRITY

EXPLORE

Choose one of these issues. What associations, stories, ideas, images, and character details do you bring to this theme? Write about how the issue has played out in your own life.

Your associations with LOVE might include experiences of betrayal, rejection, being chosen, being ecstatic, sexual and romantic awakening, fulfillment, intimacy, forming your own personal couple-world to the exclusion of others, insecurity, jealousy, commitment, celebration, going beyond your expectations and limitations, and partnership.

SUCCESS AND ACHIEVEMENT includes rejection and disappointment, being passed over, discrimination, racism and sexism, persistence, determination, ambition, greed, manipulation, control, and the desire for power.

As you observe and experience MARRIAGE and DIVORCE, you might develop an attitude that could be expressed by saying, "Marriages don't work. It's impossible for two people to live together in harmony." Or, "Marriage is about compromise."

Perhaps, as a result of a friend's marriage, you developed romantic ideas about how love should be, believing that there's one true love for each of us, and we'll know it instantly.

Perhaps, if you were ever unemployed, you learned that we need very little to get by in life. Or maybe you learned that we need a lot of money and things or we can't compete in this world. Maybe you learned when things get bad, friends and community are the only things you can depend on.

THINK

How would you prove each of these themes? How would you show that people can't live together in harmony? Or that we need little money to get by?

QUESTION

How did you come to these ideas and values? Were you struggling and your friends gave you wise advice? Did you learn from the school of hard knocks?

Did you learn by watching a negative example of how not to do it?

CONSIDER

Are there themes you would like to explore in your life, such as The Underdog Triumphs? Struggle Turns to Riches? Determination Pays Off? Write the scene you'd like to see.

REFLECT

As you look through your various life themes, write down your point of view and personal philosophy about these themes. Are you cynical? Optimistic? Idealistic? Realistic?

What forces led you to your particular philosophy? Unsupportive parents/moving too much? Feeling different? Competition with a sibling?

Once you have figured out a theme and how you feel about it, can you think of scenes from your life that exemplified that theme?

Sometimes a theme is unclear because it's muddy within the writer's mind. At other times, the writer tries to over-explain it through dialogue. Generally, you only have one or two lines to capture a character's viewpoint, so your theme has to be able to be expressed concisely.

Transforming the Theme

Have there been themes that have changed in your life? Did you once have one point of view and, a year or two later, change your opinion? If so, you went through a character arc (sometimes called a transformational journey),

which changed your attitudes, philosophical or religious
system, perhaps even your value system.

EXPLORE

To explore thematic transformations, create two
columns on a sheet of paper or in your journal. In one
column, write down an issue, such as divorce or isolation. In the other column, write down the many experiences that you've had with this issue. Has your
perception and attitude about the issue changed as
you matured?

Here's how my column might look about the issue of
Isolation.

ISSUE	I LEARNED ABOUT ISOLATION BY...
from ISOLATION to COMMUNITY	I used to think that I could "go it alone" and that the mark of a mature person was the ability to be a self-made wo/man. However, after going through years of school and training, and still having problems getting a job, I finally admitted that I couldn't do it alone and decided to hire a career consultant to see if someone could help me create a career.
	I hired Judith Claire, who helped me create and shape and develop my script-consulting career. As a result of that, I realized that there were many people who had a great deal to teach me. I hired clothes consultants and financial consultants and public-speaking consul-tants and PR consultants and developed the attitude that if there was some-thing I needed to know, probably there was someone out there who could help me.

> Soon, I began to see my life as a web of relationships. I asked advice more, spent more time developing relationships, became a more giving person as well as someone open to receiving the good gifts that others could give me.
>
> I moved from isolation to relationship.

Although this is a straightforward account, notice that implicit in the ideas above are a number of scenes that express such emotions as frustration, hardships and struggle, depression, decisions to be made, events and people who influenced and transformed me, success and relief. Working with this transformation movement, I would look for the scenes that are the most dramatic, representing the crisis points and character conflicts and internal and external struggles that I went through to reach my goal.

You can do this exercise with several different transformation themes in your life.

WRITE

Write out the series of scenes that are part of one of your transformations. Make sure the conflict and drama are clear.

YOUR SCRIPT

What character transformations occur in your script? Are they clear? How are they communicated?

Uncovering Your Value System

The ways in which we understand and interpret the themes of our lives become the foundations of our value systems.

We learn negative as well as positive values from our experiences. People who have had to struggle and feel they have little to show for it may not put much value on hard work. When love relationships don't work out, you might decide that love is really about lust and opportunity and good looks, and have little value for aspects of love such as respect and appreciation and care.

Personal themes of identity, integrity, community, love, success, and self-esteem change as we grow. How we meet all of life's challenges determines our value systems and influences our writing. The message you want to get across in your screenplay will be better defined after you clearly understand what your own values are.

Your work as a screenwriter will express your value system, whether your value system is conscious or unconscious. Your message will be clearest when you understand what your values are and can fine-tune the ideas you want to express.

VALUE CLARIFICATION EXERCISE 1

Look at the following list of values and rank them according to which is the most important to you, the second, the third, etc.

INTEGRITY
RELIGION/SPIRITUALITY
OPEN-MINDEDNESS
GENEROSITY
HONESTY
LOYALTY
INTUITION

Do you think loyalty is more important than honesty? Is spirituality more important than integrity? Do you prefer people who are open-minded to people who are intuitive?

VALUES CLARIFICATION EXERCISE 2

Below are two great scandals of the 1990s. Both have a large cast of characters. You decide who the good guys and bad guys are.

The O.J. Simpson Case

O.J. Simpson (Victim or manipulator?)

Judge Ito (Methodical or disorganized?)

Marcia Clark (A high-profile victory for women or an example of a woman promoted beyond her abilities?)

Johnny Cochran (Showman or devoted attorney?)

Barry Scheck (A man of integrity or a sell-out for money?)

Christopher Darden (A token black or a competent professional?)

Mark Furhman (Racist or victim?)

Kato (Movie star or opportunist?)

The Press (Manipulators or truth-tellers?)

People who wrote books about Simpson and the trial (Cashing in on tragedy or revealing the truth?)

THINK

List some of the themes that came out of this case:

THE FALLEN HERO

RACISM

MANIPULATION

EQUALITY FOR WOMEN AND BLACKS

TRUTH

JUSTICE OR INJUSTICE

WEALTH AND PRIVILEGE

SENSATIONALISM

REALITY VS. PERCEPTION

List some of the questions and underlying ideas that were part of this case, such as:

Is it better to let 100 guilty men go free than to wrongly imprison one innocent man?

Does the adversarial positioning of the prosecution and defense serve justice?

Can a "not guilty" verdict be purchased?

WRITE

Write a scene that you remember from the case—a courtroom scene, a murder scene, O.J.'s escape in the Bronco, or an investigation scene.

Do you sympathize with the prosecution or the defense in the courtroom scene? Do you show a getaway from the point of view of an uncertain witness or the callous murderer?

Show your value system by the approach you take to the scene.

VALUES CLARIFICATION EXERCISE 3

Look at another scandal from the 1990s. Rank the players and the values.

The Clinton-Lewinsky Scandal

According to your value system, is adultery worse than betrayal? Is justice more important than forgiveness? How important is truth to you? Who's telling it? Whose behavior do you think is the worst?

President Clinton (Adulterer using the power of his office to seduce a young woman? Is he a man gone astray and wronged?)

Linda Tripp (Betrayer or seeker after justice?)

Lucianne Goldberg (Opportunist or great businesswoman?)

Monica Lewinsky (Perpetrator, victim, opportunist, or slut?)

Kenneth Starr (Witch-hunter or relentless pursuer of
  truth and justice?)
Hilary Rodham Clinton (Wife betrayed? Loyal wife?
  Diplomat? A woman who will forgive/forget anything,
  as long as they can remain in the White House?)

THINK

What themes are implicit in this scandal?

ENTRAPMENT
DESPERATE FOR LOVE AND POWER
STAND BY HER MAN
A WITCH-HUNT
THE SEARCH FOR JUSTICE
MIDDLE-AGED, LUST-CRAZY MAN

WRITE

Write some of the scenes from this third scandal,
making sure that your approach to the scene con-
veys your point of view and your values.

CAST THE ROLES

Decide which actors would best express and project
your point of view. Who will play Clinton? John
Travolta (à la *Primary Colors*) or Ray Liotta? Who will
play Monica? A young Glen Close (à la *Fatal
Attraction*) or Cameron Diaz or Winona Ryder?
What qualities in the actor help you convey your
point of view?

IMAGINE

Take these scandals and combine them to see
whether a new combination would better express
your point of view. What if O.J. were accused of having sex with an NBC intern? What if Hillary had a

lover, and Bill Clinton killed him? What if Hillary killed
Monica? What other combinations can you think of?

WRITE SOME MORE

Explore other scandals. Create the characters.
Write a scene. Cast the script.

Theme saturates a film. It's in the action. It's in the way
the characters act and respond. It's in the dialogue. Hopefully it's always in the images. How do you visualize a
theme? By becoming a visual- and sensation-thinker.

6.

Mastering the Skill of
Sensation-Thinking

What do you remember after you've seen a film? Do you remember people having chats in a car? People getting to know each other over coffee? People sharing their life stories while walking down a street? With the exception of a very few, rather unusual, films, probably not.

Great films by great writers are filled with sensation—sounds, images that can haunt us for years, colors, and visuals.

Think about a scene from a film that has left its mark on your memory. Perhaps it's the scene from *Gone With the Wind* when Scarlett desperately looks for a doctor for Melanie among thousands of wounded soldiers spread out as far as the eye can see. Or perhaps it's the vast desert in *Lawrence of Arabia*, with the boy who is sucked to his death by the spiraling sands.

It might be the first act of *Saving Private Ryan*—the blood that has turned the sea to red and the cacophony of war, with shells pinging and wounded men screaming.

Perhaps you remember the floating bodies at the end of *Titanic* or the winding line of headlights in *Field of Dreams*.

Who chooses these cinematic images? You, the writer. If you haven't written the scene, the director can't shoot the scene. The great screenwriter is able to imagine the look of the sets and scenes—the images, the sounds, the movement of the characters, the energy of the action, the feel of the scene, the tactile textures that are part of the character's environment. Although all of these sensations will be further developed by the director, set designer, and costumer, the more trained you are to think through your senses, the more cinematic your scripts will become. If your script is highly visual, directors will more easily see your work as a film, not as a play. Actors will see new levels to the characters. Producers will want to do your work because you understand the medium of film.

Sensation-thinking can be learned with practice. You may already be a vivid visual thinker but find that you don't think in sounds. Or perhaps you can see the film as you write it, but don't yet think in visual metaphors. Maybe you're more of a feeling type—you can intuit your characters, but don't know how to bring sense-awareness to your work. Maybe you're an auditory person, but don't know how to use feeling and touch to enrich your work. The exercises in this chapter are designed to train your senses so that you can bring your sense perceptions to the scenes you write.

As you do the following exercises, be aware of what comes naturally and what presents problems. If they all come easily, great.

Working With Visual Thinking

In the 1970s, I spent two years exploring my own creative process. One of the most helpful books I found was *Adventures in Visual Thinking* by Robert McKim, who created many exercises to help readers develop their ability to think visually. Some of this chapter revises his exercises,

moving from his artistic and scientific focus to the visual-
izations necessary for the screenwriter.

Begin by seeing how easily you visualize objects, and
where the visualization becomes difficult.

> Visualize a black car. Make it a specific car—your
> own, a VW bug, a BMW, or any car you want. Can you
> see it clearly? Is it a vague image or a clear image?
> Focus on it with your mind's eye. If it's not yet clear,
> it will become clear with some practice.

> Visualize the same car in pink. Then in yellow. Now
> the car is blue. Now it's purple.

> Visualize the car half green and half magenta. How
> does that work for you? Is it still clear? Or has this
> strange and unnatural exercise muddied up your
> vision?

> If you're having trouble visualizing, go outside and
> look at your own car. Study it. Close your eyes and
> imagine your car. Open your eyes and study it again.
> Then notice other cars. Keep moving back and forth
> between seeing and imagining.

> Next, visualize the car moving. Watch it on the free-
> way. On the mountain road. Watch it drive along the
> ocean. Got it? Did the movement present any
> problems?

If you had trouble with any of these images, don't worry,
just keep practicing.

> Tomorrow, visualize a house. The next day, visualize a
> kangaroo and change its colors. The next day, see a
> brown road, a purple road, and the yellow brick road.
> Make up visuals.

Visualize a familiar face.

This, for some reason, is the most difficult exercise for me. But as a writer, you'll want to be able to do this. Some writers say it helps them create the character to think of Goldie Hawn playing a part, or Meg Ryan or Tommy Lee Jones or Anthony Hopkins. Visualizing an actor or a type of look will also help you decide where to send your script. Should you send it to Oprah Winfrey's production company or to Rosie O'Donnell's? By being flexible with your thinking, you might decide that either woman could play the lead, and you'll send it to both.

Visualize events from your past. Last night's dinner, last year's vacation, your favorite birthday party.

When I first started working on my visual thinking, I had trouble with objects in motion—such as the galloping horse, the flying bird, the track star running past the finish line. They seemed to move in fits and starts, almost like stop-motion. If you're encountering that problem, keep practicing.

Using visual thinking, you'll be able to change your mind as you write—changing the color and style of the house, the style of clothes your character wears, imagining your protagonist as male, then female, as a different race, or from a different culture. Combine your flexible thinking with your ability to think visually in order to experiment with dramatic alternatives.

YOUR SCRIPT

Visualize a scene from your story. How cinematic and vibrant and uniquely visual is the scene? Try making it more visual by changing the location or adding color or giving it more action.

Imagine the Uncomfortable

Next, work with images that may be uncomfortable. As a writer, you need to be able to allow your visual thinking to lead you to emotional imagination.

IMAGINE

To train yourself to work with uncomfortable images, begin by imagining a fish called Wanda. Watch her swim around in the aquarium. Now, imagine picking her up, putting her into your mouth, and letting her swim down your esophagus and into your stomach, swishing around a bit down there. Imagine Wanda having a good time swimming around in your colorful gastric juices. Then breathe her out. Did it feel disgusting? Frightening? Rather cute? Imagine drinking bleach, cutting your finger with a sharp knife, trying to hop a train, and not making it.

If an image is uncomfortable, just let it be. When I first started to work with these exercises, I resented them and found them terribly uncomfortable. By breathing, calming myself down, and working with them for several days in a row, their negative energy dissipated and I could begin to both see and feel the images. You want to push your discomfort level so that you can deal with uncomfortable material in your scripts and create the full context and emotional atmosphere of the scene.

Do certain ideas terrify you? Perhaps someone breaking into your home or being crippled or being trapped? Think of an uncomfortable image, and stay with it. Breathe it in and out and be conscious of your feelings about it.

If you're going to do a shoot-'em-up action-adventure, you'll need to see the bullets flying and feel the fear of the hero as he desperately tries to hide or escape from certain death.

If you're going to write a movie about war, you'll have to write about the terror of battle. You will have to decide just how horrifying you need your scenes to be. Visualize yourself in the midst of war. Soldiers are dying all around you. Some of them cringe in fear, others scream in agony as they're shot. Perhaps you're the medic. Perhaps you're the one who fired the shot. Perhaps you're the one who's dying. Perhaps you're brave. Perhaps you're terrified. Do you show the fear or hide it so others won't think less of you?

IMAGINE

Visualize yourself in a situation that terrifies you and makes you shudder. As you visualize, be deeply aware of your feelings as though you have to report everything you're going through to your counselor.

Make the images more personal. See if you can imagine and remember uncomfortable scenes from your life. First, remember. Then visualize. Now, utilizing your memories and your visual thinking, see the details. Where were you? Who was with you? What did people say? Then let the images move into your emotional life until your body actually remembers what your mind is thinking.

CREATE

Try to create a battle scene that is not stereotypical but emotionally powerful. To do this, combine your memory of times you felt fear with your knowledge (no matter how small) of battle and war. Visualize several different kinds of scenes, seeing which scenes awaken the most fear in you. Write them down.

In Chapter Four, when I remembered and visualized my experience with Gail on the mountain, I could feel my fear, my shock at realizing we were in such a mess, my fight for clear-headedness, my desperation as I sought for a way out of what seemed hopeless. When I think of the situation, I begin to feel tightness in my arms, constricted breath, fear behind my eyes. I remember that I had just rented a new apartment and felt sad that I probably would never live there.

WRITE

> When the uncomfortable image seems clear enough, write it out as a scene. See if you can capture the visuals and the feelings.

You can also use your ability to work through uncomfortable images by changing them from emotionally charged images to playful images.

During the 1970s, a creativity book, *Put Your Mother On The Ceiling* by Richard De Mille, was published. It was written for children, to help them deal with difficult situations by diffusing the power that adults sometimes lorded over them. If the children felt afraid of Mom, they imagined her on the ceiling, which dispelled their fear. This is a good exercise, particularly for screenwriters who may need to get past rejection by imagining Michael Eisner in the bathroom hamper, Stephen Spielberg inside a blow-up Betty Boop doll, and all the executives of MGM on a trampoline.

As you become more comfortable with the uncomfortable images mentioned above, make up some more and practice working with them. Notice your discomfort level. When you hit it, breathe deeply and practice concentrating on the image until you can work with it.

Notice if there are uncomfortable images in the stories that you're writing. How many different ways can you visualize an image? If it's a fire in a building, how much fear do you want to show? How much panic? At what point do you become uncomfortable with your images? Is this discomfort necessary for your audience?

If the mother is sick, how sick is she? Is she wasting away? Is she having difficulty talking? Having halluci- nations?

Working with uncomfortable images will also help you do the research necessary to make your characters ring true. If you're going to deal with death in your script, then you need to know what death looks like. By first visualiz- ing what you know about death, you can dissipate your discomfort and make it possible for you to do the neces- sary research—whether that's going to a morgue, visiting the terminally ill wing of a hospital, or sitting in on an autopsy. Once you have your research materials, you can then decide how horrific to make the image. You'll be in- formed, because you're basing your image on fact. And you'll be responsible, because you're considering various images and deciding which image best communicates the drama without turning off the audience.

You might feel uncomfortable writing certain scenes because you want to be considered a writer who writes uplifting stories. In her book *The Practice of Poetry*, Lynn Emanuel suggests the following exercise to help you for- get your good manners and tell the truth:

Grandma (or someone else you know) is dying. Rather than being sentimental and maudlin about it, consider the truth about the situation, even if it's uncomfortable. Maybe, secretly, you'll be relieved when she finally goes. Maybe you want to feel pity but you only feel gratitude that it's not you. Maybe she is small and mean-spirited. Maybe her bravery surprises you and fills you with guilt.[1] Maybe, when grandma dies, it's not raining and the trees aren't bare but the sun shines and the world is rather happy to get rid of her.[2]

Notice how you felt as you read that last sentence. It al- most made me shiver to write it, because my grandmas were wonderful people, and their deaths were sad to me. But not all grandmas are terrific, and maybe you're going to do a story where you need to present that shuddering truth about some grandmas. Emanuel recommends that you tell the truth, even though your subconscious, which has spent years protecting you from unpleasantries, may object.

We often write with the fear that our mother or our minister/priest/rabbi will read what we write. Their voices in our heads can detain us from telling the truth in all its complexity. This doesn't mean that I recommend searing images that cause nightmares and have no dramatic use. But this is a call for flexible thinking combined with responsible choices.

YOUR SCRIPT

Do you have any uncomfortable images in your script? If not, why not? Might you be shying away from exploring an important image that's essential to the drama?

Working With Your Other Senses

Just as your mind's eye can visualize images, it can also imagine other sensations. Can you hear the sound of rain on a tin roof? It's a sound you'd want to be able to imagine if you were writing a script like *Rain*. Can you hear the ping of bullets? You'd need to hear that sound if you're writing *Boyz N the Hood*. Can you imagine the roar of engines at the race track? You'd want to if you were writing *Heart Like a Wheel* or *Thunder*. If you were writing *Wait Until Dark*, you'd need to imagine the importance of sounds to a blind woman.

Imagine the wind in the trees. Imagine the sound when someone dives into water. Imagine the meow of your cat or the bark of your dog. Imagine the sound of a waterfall. Imagine the dripping of a faucet.

If you had trouble with one of these images, such as the dripping faucet, go to the bathroom and turn it on and let it drip, drip, drip. Now, turn it off, and try to remember the sound. Hear it in your head. As I was writing this, I was having trouble with that sound. I turned on the faucet but couldn't get it to drip, only to whir. But I noticed, as the water whirred out of the spout, it gurgled as it went down the drain. It was difficult to hold both sounds in my mind. So I worked on the sounds sequentially—first the whir, then the gurgle. Now, imagine how you might use these sounds in a screenplay.

Sense Out Your House

ACT

Walk around your home and check it out for sounds. Turn on the stove. Listen to your footsteps. Hear someone in the next room. Slam doors. Close doors softly. Check out the heating and air conditioning system. Turn your lights on and off. Throw a few books on the floor. See if you can create at least five sounds in each room. Then stop and hear those sounds in your mind.

The screenwriter will make more cinematic scripts when s/he also pays attention to other non-visual senses. Smell and taste are not usually important parts of a film. But occasionally, smell or taste has led to the discovery of death by poison or finding a decomposing body. And the smell of smoke has meant fire!

In *Dead Poets Society*, you may remember when Neil's father comes into the room after Neil has killed himself. The father stops, smells the gunshot, turns, sees the gun and his son's hand, and then sees his son. Smell became an important sensation in the scene, and smell moved the father into the discovery of his dead son.

Have you ever noticed how many films have people eating, but we rarely see them react to their food's smells and tastes? They rarely respond to the smell of fresh-brewed coffee served over a campfire or the smell of fresh-baked cinnamon rolls or the taste of a martini. Of course, you don't want to slow down your story by having everyone smell and taste, but watch some eating scenes in movies. When do the characters respond to what they're eating? When don't they? Which is more dramatically interesting? (Some movies with eating scenes include *Age of Innocence, Diner, Remains of the Day, Like Water for Chocolate, Babette's Feast, Big Night, Tom Jones, My Dinner with André The Cook the Thief His Wife & Her Lover*.)

Feel, Touch, Become a Sensualist

Although seeing and hearing are the screenwriter's most-used senses, expanding your ability to be aware of the sense of touch can help make your film more colorful, richer, and more identifiable. The sense of touch can be used to express the transformation of a character who may move from isolation (cut off from the feeling of things as well as people) to intimacy. Touch can show the character's increasing connection to the world outside herself, as the character first hugs herself, running her fingers over the soft wool of her sweater. Perhaps she then feels the water running over her hand, then puts her head on his shoulder, feeling the rough corduroy of his jacket collar, and then feels the fresh sheets and a juicy kiss as they make love.

ACT

Walk around your home and be aware of its surfaces. Are they hard or soft? Textured? Rough? Smooth? Imagine putting more textures into your home. How might you change your bedroom? Plush blankets, perhaps fleece? Satin sheets? A terry-cloth robe?

Come up with at least ten textures that you could add to your bedroom. Do the same with your kitchen, your den, your livingroom, even your bathroom. Go for quantity of ideas here. Stretch yourself. Begin feeling the rooms.

Create a Love Scene

In the following exercises, work further with the quantity of ideas, remembering that the creative mind often finds quality and originality after getting past the obvious.

CREATE

Create a love scene, using all your senses. Set the stage. ninety percent of the people reading this book will probably have candles. That's fine. But just for fun, blow out the candles, and try out five other kinds of romantic light sources.

Start the love scene in the living room. Okay, you probably have a fire lit. That's fine. But snuff out the fire and see what else you can use for the heat and fire of romance.

Think of romantic foods. Did you think of strawberries and figs? If so, take them back to the kitchen and come back with ten other romantic foods that are luscious and sensual. Make a love feast. Be unconventional.

What about textures? Did you think of velvet and velour and plush fleece? If so, put them back in the closet and bring out five other romantic textures that you could use.

Be playful with this. Bring out the Christmas tree lights if you must, or the Donald Duck lantern. Did you ever notice how serious everyone is about love in the movies? Be truthful—don't you sometimes use humor when you're being romantic in real life? Be spontaneous. Have fun with what you add.

Now, they're not allowed to go to bed in this scene. They are going to be intimate, but no sex. (That's a new one for Hollywood, isn't it?) See if you can use all the senses to make this a rich and intimate love scene. Think of what they say, the sound of their voices, the sounds in the background, the way they feel the textures because they're still shy about touching each other. Let the scene build and move and develop. Don't forget any of the senses.

Go back and play out another love scene, but set this one in the dining room. Then set one on the porch. Then the kitchen. The basement. The attic. The garage. In each scene, let the sensations that you choose reinforce the atmosphere that you're developing.

If you want them to go to bed, move them to the bedroom, but keep working with your senses as you construct the love scene. Go ahead, create a romantic, beautiful, sensual love scene in the bedroom without doing anything conventional.

Instead of reinforcing the scene with a romantic atmosphere, work with oppositions. Your characters are still madly in love, but the sensations around them are not reinforcing that feeling. Instead of soft candlelight, maybe the overhead light is glaring, the sound next door is the neighbor practicing the

trumpet badly, a siren goes past, the tea kettle
goes off at the most inopportune moment, and the
only thing they have to eat are pretzels, left over
from the airplane trip. Work against type, while using
your senses.

YOUR SCRIPT

How might you use these techniques to make your
love scenes more sensual and more original?

Creating Visual Metaphors

In the film *Il Postino*, poet Pablo Neruda tries to explain
metaphors to Mario, the postman. What is a metaphor?
"When you talk of something, comparing it to another,"
explains Neruda. "Will they come to me, these metaphors?"
asks Mario, who wants to be a poet. "Certainly," says Neruda.
As Mario listens to Neruda's poetry, he suddenly finds himself talking in metaphors, saying, "I felt like a boat tossing
around on your words." "You've invented a metaphor." "No,"
says Mario. "Yes," says Neruda. "No, really? But it doesn't
count because I didn't mean to." And then Mario suggests
a possibility—"The whole world is a metaphor for something else."[3]

Metaphor is more than just description. We can read many
books that describe the magenta wallpaper in the room, the
purple color and velvet texture of the dress, the green rolling hills, or the blue of the Mediterranean. Metaphors, however, carry meanings and associations that remind us of like,
and even unlike, ideas. They add emotional resonance, allowing us to feel a movie, not just watch a film.

Thinking in metaphor is far more natural than we
might expect. We speak of "feeling blue," of "being a bit
edgy," of "reaching a dead end" in our lives, of being "all
mixed up." One of my friends told me that when he was

very ill he felt that Death was hovering, tracking him, waiting to capture him. When we work with metaphors, we borrow a visual image to better communicate our state of mind.

In the film *The Rose*, Bette Midler sings about certain metaphors of love, including a river, a razor, a hunger, and a rose.

BRAINSTORM

Take each of these metaphors and brainstorm all the different ways that love is a river, a razor, a hunger, a rose. Can you think of new images that could be a metaphor for the different aspects of love? Does the metaphor change if love is a raging, out-of-control flood? If love is an orchid rather than a rose?

In screenwriting, metaphors are used as images that represent an idea. For instance, if I describe someone as "a steamroller," you understand the image and act accordingly. Steamrollers press down, flatten out. The image creates unconscious associations in your mind that make you feel that you would be oppressed, not free to be yourself, in this person's presence. Now imagine a film about the theme of oppression vs. freedom. What if the main oppressive character drove a steamroller for a living? A bit on the nose, right? But it would carry the association of oppression if you saw that image connected to a character who is oppressive in other ways. Now make the image more subtle. Perhaps the person is a contractor and there's a steamroller working in the background. Or perhaps your protagonist who desires to be free always walks to school past a construction site with tractors and steamrollers and crushing dumptrucks.

Metaphor recognizes that images have meaning. They represent and symbolize ideas. If I asked, "What does integrity look like?" you might think of images from *To Kill a Mockingbird*. Think of how *The Fugitive* lets images speak about captivity by focusing on handcuffs, bars, and leg irons. What does freedom look like? Watch *Titanic*, as Rose and Jack stand with arms spread wide to catch the wind on the prow of the ship.

Could you image the search for meaning? *A Room with a View* does it, showing George forming his vegetables into question marks.

In the film *Beloved*, the character of Beloved works as a metaphor. She appears in the front yard of the home of Sethe (Oprah Winfrey), who is haunted by guilt because she killed her child years before. Beloved is dirty, has bad manners, is child-like and strange, and brings darkness and anguish into a house that already seems haunted by an evil presence. By the end of the film, Beloved's meaning is clear—she is the dead child, the guilt, the unresolved past, the curse of the sins of the mother, the spirit that takes away life.

Alfred Hitchcock used fresh metaphors in his films. He recounts the metaphor used in one of his silent films, *The Ring*. "The young boxer comes home after winning his fight. He's flushed with success—wants to celebrate. He pours out champagne all round. Then he finds out his wife is out, and he knows at once that she is out with another man. At this moment, the camera cuts to a glass of champagne; you see of a fizz of bubbles rise off it, and there it stands untasted, going flat. That one shot gives you the whole feeling of the scene."[4]

IMAGINE

Use color, space, props, and setting to represent such themes as freedom, justice, and ambition. Create scenes with these themes.

Visualize war or death or justice or greed. Free-associate. If freedom reminds you of somebody riding in convertible, then what's the next image you see? Riding along the ocean? And the next? Climbing out of the basement? And the next? Flowers reaching up to the sun?

Don't be concerned if the images don't make sense. Let the images erupt in your mind. Let them pop up, even if they're non sequiturs. If freedom means eating a whole closet-full of figs, then explore that image. See where it leads you. Try to come up with at least five images that make no sense. Then see if there's anything usable in them.

YOUR SCRIPT

What fresh metaphors do you work with in your script? Which metaphors are you using that might be overused? Can you change them to make them more original?

Image Can Follow Function

We've already learned that themes beget images. Now use images to beget themes. You can start this process by thinking of an object—such as a mirror. What does this object mean? A mirror can reflect reality, be used to send a signal by reflecting the sun, be ground up and used as sharp glass, be used to show one's vanity. A mirror can also crack, break, and distort.[5] If you use the image of a mirror to tell us something about a character, you must decide what function that mirror has as a metaphor for that character. Does your character reflect the light of others but hasn't found her own identity? Is your character falling to pieces? Does your character always distort the truth? As your character changes, how might the function of the object also change?

BRAINSTORM

Think of an object, such as water, which often symbolizes the unconscious or emotions. How can you change the water's form to change the metaphor? For instance, what kind of character or idea would be imaged through a baptismal font? A raging river? A glass of Perrier? A mud puddle? Frost on the windowpane?

Think of a diamond. How could it be used to symbolize a theme of greed? Integrity? Illusion? Fame? Fortune? Corruption?

Look around your home or walk around the neighborhood and choose five to ten other objects and brainstorm how a theme could change depending on how you use the object.

Look at how your favorite films work with objects. I particularly like the use of images in *The Last Emperor*. The film uses images of curtains and cloths and doors and screens to show the separation that existed between the emperor and his people, his bride, and other cultures.

How would you symbolize the idea of life and death? Dying vs. healing? Make your list, then watch *The English Patient* to see how Anthony Minghella worked with wet (moist, nourishing) and dry (dying, decaying) images to show the juxtaposition of these ideas—the desert vs. the cave painting of swimmers. The fact that it rained on the day that the war was over. Or that the dying man begged for water and was covered with wet cloths to help heal his burns. Katherine loves Cairo for its plumbing. She takes constant baths. Cairo (associated with wet and nourishing images) is where the affair began between the Count and Katherine.

Other films that are rich in metaphoric images include:

The Piano
Unforgiven
The Terminator
The Thin Red Line
Alien
Cousin Bette
Eve's Bayou
Like Water for Chocolate

Using Images to Transform Character

Metaphors can symbolize a character's transformation. As the character changes, the metaphors also change to show the transformation.

You've heard the expression "a rolling stone gathers no moss." In it original meaning, it refers to a drifter going through life, never staying long enough to pick up any friends or associations or loves. But I adopt this saying to speak of metaphor as a rolling snowball that gathers moss and dried leaves and all sorts of other associations as it moves through a script. Think of the rolling snowball as your central idea that travels through your story, picking up meaning and new images continually.

The best example I've found of this "rolling snowball" moving through the script is the grain image from the movie *Witness*. Each time we see it, it carries new associations. We see it first in the wheat, waving in the wind at the Amish farm—a symbol of peace and harmony. Then, we see it as fresh-baked bread, organic to the Amish community. We also see it in the processed hot-dog bun that John Book eats and in the flour where the bullets are hidden. Later it's corn from the silo that kills Fergie.

Each time the visual metaphor appears in the film, the grain is shown as being corrupted, processed, changed from its natural harmonious state, in the same way that the community has been changed, even corrupted, when John Book brings violence into its peaceful world.

CREATE

Describe a character through the use of a metaphor. You might find it helpful to start with yourself, or to use these images about someone you know.

"I am" or "my girlfriend/boyfriend is" or "my father is"

a clinging vine,
a bulldozer,
a prickly pear,
a big Mac truck,
the fallow land.[6]

In what way does the image fit the character? How would you visualize this with your character? Prove the statement through an image.

Now, let's say that your character is going to change from a clinging vine to a pine tree on the hill, so she's going to move from dependent to independent.

IMAGINE

What images would you show to clarify this transformation? The character would have to begin with strong images of her clinging and being dependent, perhaps hanging on her boyfriend. Maybe she lives in a house with climbing wisteria and vines. Maybe she has photographs of her boyfriend all over the house. Maybe her clothes twirl around her, like a clinging vine. Then, find an image that shows her beginning to untangle herself and stretch out a bit. Maybe she asks to drive his convertible. Maybe she starts dressing differently—wearing jeans or clothes that allow more movement. Maybe you work with images of animals that represent her transformation—she gets an independent cat after her dependent dog dies. Maybe her boyfriend dies or she breaks up with him, and at the end she's by herself, swimming in the ocean, free from earth, with nothing clinging to her.

Keep thinking of images that can clarify a transformation. In most scripts, a transformation will require anywhere from ten to twenty story beats to prove that the character has really changed. (A story beat is any event or action in a script that develops or propels the story. A story might have fifty to two-hundred story beats. A subplot might have three to fifty story beats.) Write twenty different changing images to show the transformational process.

Now change the character from a female to a male. Does the image change? Is it more dramatically interesting?

Try out other transformations:

From a Kmart sundress to a Dior original, from a big Mac truck to a humming VW bug, from dark to light.

Keep the metaphor moving. If your character gains freedom by the end of your script, s/he might start in tight, small spaces that gradually become bigger as your images and theme develop.

In *Good Will Hunting*, writers Ben Affleck and Matt Damon use small spaces to begin Will's journey toward freedom, ending with the open road on the way to California. Although the images could have been developed further to show Will's growth, the final image does the job.

RECORD

In your notebook, record real-life situations that express a theme.

I saw the following image of freedom when I was teaching in Stockholm in 1998. I was in an elevator when a little boy got in with his parents. His father pushed the button for the twelfth floor. When the elevator stopped at the fifth floor to let someone off, the little boy tried to get out. His parents grabbed him, holding him back, and he started to cry. The elevator stopped at the ninth floor and more people got off. Again, the boy tried to get off the elevator and, again, his parents held him back, trying to explain that this was not yet their floor. When the elevator finally stopped at the twelfth floor, the little boy cried again because he didn't want to get off. They almost had to drag him out of the elevator. This was an excellent example of wanting freedom, but when the opportunity to be free finally presented itself, he didn't want it anymore. What is the emotion behind such a change of mind? Fear? Anticipation of the vast, chaotic unknown beyond the safety of our smaller space? I saw the image, associated it with a theme, then interpreted the image in terms of a meaning.

CREATE

Use my story and complicate the image. Just as the previous image of the little boy started out as a freedom image, but then told us about the ambiguity of freedom, find some images that work with opposition between the theme and the image. We feel

torn between freedom vs. connection or space vs.
closeness or integrity vs. success or intimacy vs.
solitude. Although these are not always mutually
exclusive, we think they are, and the images sometimes represent the fight that we are experiencing.

To show this contradiction, you might have an image of
a very tight-lipped and tightly dressed woman in a convertible—who is belying the freedom image of the speeding
car and therefore dimensionalizing the character and shading the theme that image is portraying.

It might be the high-powered speed boat that can't get
going because the motor keeps giving out.

It might be the road that looks like it's going over the
horizon, but suddenly ends at a cliff or a dead end or in a
squatter's town or a hobo's village.

ACT

Look around your home or go for a walk or visit a mall
and try to find at least ten objects that could have
thematic meaning—perhaps a swimming pool, a
blooming rose, the tabby cat, a piece of string, the
vibrating chair, a lost penny, etc. Articulate the
themes that the images might represent. Then complicate the images and complicate the themes. How
would the theme change if the rose dies, the
swimming pool is empty and decaying, the string is a
ball of yarn, the cat has a thorn in her paw?

You might paint or draw or storyboard these scenes to
see if that process gives you more visual ideas.

Explore the Image Through Film

THINK

How would you image the idea of tradition vs. individuality? Or creativity vs. conformity?

After you make your list, watch *Dead Poets Society* and look at the many images the film uses to show tradition and conformity vs. freedom and creativity and individuality. Notice the first scene that images tradition through the use of candles, the procession, the stately welcoming ceremony. Later, Keating helps the boys find their individuality by encouraging them to march out of step with each other.

ANALYZE

Watch the film and look for at least ten other images that show tradition and conformity vs. individuality and creativity. I guarantee that you'll find them.

BRAINSTORM

How would you image the idea of tyranny vs. liberation?

After you make your list, watch *One Flew Over The Cuckoo's Nest* to see all the different ways that images work in opposition to each other to convey the theme. Notice the tyranny of order and control—when to watch television, how to act in group meetings, when to take pills, versus McMurphy's spontaneity expressed through throwing butter on the wall, wearing humorous underwear, taking the guys out on a boat. Notice how the neckbrace that Nurse Ratched wears shows that liberation has crippled tyranny. Look for other images.

ANALYZE

Study and research images from films, asking what they mean. Use them as jumping-off places for your own creativity, adding to them, changing them, moving them in new directions.

Discovering Your Responses to Your Senses

When I took Creative Drama in college, we were asked to keep a sense diary. Every day, we wrote down at least one entry for each of our five senses. It was one of the best exercises I've done to teach me to sit up and notice what's going on around me.

Buy a small notebook, and for the next week or month or six months, record an entry for each of your senses and see how this will awaken you as a writer and as a person. Notice what you choose, what excites you, what you find intriguing and fascinating.

Train yourself to notice. Observe. Take it in. And then use your senses to create rich cinematic scripts.

7.

Mining the Riches From
Your Dreams

As a child, were you ever told, "Don't be such a dreamer"?
Did you ever wonder if dreaming was at odds with making
a living? The good news is that most great screenwriters
gain a wealth of ideas from their night dreams and their
daydreams.

During our waking life, we adapt to our logical rational
world and fit in just fine. We move in patterns, do what's
expected, keep our temper, and feel in control.

In our dream life, we scream and shout, do odd and impossible things, feel afraid and alienated, have highly
charged erotic relationships with all kinds of unsuitable
lovers, perform acts of courage, try to escape from wild
animals and flying objects and people intent on finding us
and chasing us.

Guess where the high drama is? If you're missing your
dreams, you're missing the good stuff.

If you, as a writer, bypass your own personal life by only
modeling your characters after people you see around you,
or worse, modeling them after characters you see in the
movies, they most likely will lack subtext. Your ability to
access your unconscious can help give emotional truth to

your characters, provide you with new ideas, work you through writing blocks, and provide you with colorful and powerful images. Understanding and acknowledging the many strange and disturbing and original worlds within you can provide fertile ground for your work.

How can you consciously get at what is unconscious? To begin, learn to value and remember your dreams. Secondly, treat your dreams as an inexhaustible creative resource that you can mine for images, story ideas, emotional tones, and insights.

You can map out a way into your dreams through your dream journal.

Keep a Dream Journal

The fleeting nature of dreams often causes them to be quickly forgotten upon waking. You need to be prepared to capture these elusive images. Thoughts flow at night because your conscious mind isn't able to guard the gates to these strange worlds. Therefore, a little stream or a flood of images can pop out, unchecked.

To capture your dreams, keep a notebook or tape recorder by your bed and record your dreams every morning. If it's difficult to remember dreams, do the following exercise every night:

> Let your unconscious know you're serious about remembering. Before going to sleep, open your dream journal and date it for the next morning. If it's Saturday night, December 20th, date it for Sunday Morning, December 21st. Then go to sleep. If you wake up from a dream, write it down.

You have now told your unconscious that you want to remember your dreams. You've made a commitment to recording them. Considering that we dream every ninety minutes, each night we have five or six different possible stories, images, emotions, insights, that can be usable for creative work.

The next morning, if you wake up and know you've been dreaming but can't remember what you dreamed, roll over and let your mind wander to see if it can catch the dream. If it doesn't come, roll over to the other side, and see if it comes.

If you've been dreaming on your right side and roll over onto your left side, it's easy to lose the dream. By rolling back and taking a few minutes to look for dream snippets, some memory of your dream should come within five or ten minutes.

Do this exercise every night. Value any image that comes to you, no matter how small. Within a week, you should be able to remember your dreams.

Start Dream Folders

Your dreams will fall into various genres—romances, adventures, mysteries, dramas, horror stories.

Jot down powerful dreams you remember from your past. Record your current dreams.

File these dreams by categories in folders with such labels as:

Traveling Images and Journey Dreams
Movie-Star or Famous-People Dreams
Disaster Dreams
Alienation Dreams (feeling left out, being lonely)
Anxiety Dreams (trying to call someone, trying to finish an exam)

Childhood Dreams (home, places where you grew up,
    childhood friends)
Romantic Dreams
Naked Dreams/Exposure Dreams
Flying Dreams (One of my recurring dreams used to be
    about an airplane flying under high-tension wires. A
    psychologist told me that I probably felt that I
    couldn't soar. When I started taking karate lessons,
    the dreams stopped.)
Scary Dreams
Animal Dreams (snakes or monsters or being chased by
    bears, etc.)
Elevator Dreams (Have you ever dreamed that the eleva-
    tor went up too high? I have.)

Just as you have file folders to organize your waking
observations, dream folders can help you remember and
access the potential stories, images, and characters that
come out of your unconscious.

You can also add to your ability to work with dreams
by watching films that portray the world of the unconscious, such as *The Last Wave*, *The Fisher King*, *Total Re-
call*, *Flatliners*, *Jacob's Ladder*, *Nightmare on Elm Street*,
Kurosawa's *Dreams*, and many of Bergman's films. Could
any of your dreams be used in a film in the same way these
films draw on dream images?

Feeling Your Dreams

Although the individual scenes and characters in your
dreams can be usable for your stories, the emotions in your
dreams can be one of the most important elements for
deepening your characters.

It's little wonder that so many scripts lack emotion. We're
told, "Whatever you do, don't cry at work!" "Don't get angry,
or he'll never date you again." "Just calm down!" We've
learned to tame our emotions. To temper them. I've often

felt that the lack of emotional richness in so many characters comes from being out of touch with our emotional lives. As a result, characters become either overly staid or melodramatic.

Some years ago, my cousin Nancy explained to me that there are five emotions: mad, sad, glad, hurt, and scared. These easily become muted in our lives. We are trained to subdue our ecstasy, take pills to get over our sadness, hide our hurt, clench our teeth so we don't show fear, and to never show anger.

Movies give us an opportunity to see characters who desire madly, love passionately, care deeply, respond fully. Our dream life is usually lived with this same intensity. That's what you want to capture in your work.

The book *Dreaming and Waking* by Hart, Corriere, Karle, and Woldenberg recommends that upon waking from a dream, you ask yourself, "How do I feel in this dream?"[1] Do I feel ecstatic? Alienated? Confused? Bewildered? Sad? Excited? Aroused? Energized? Was I terrified? Threatened? Was there danger? Rivalry?[2]

WRITE

When you record your dreams, include the emotions. If you can't remember a dream, write down how you feel upon waking. *Dreaming* and *Waking* recommends making up a dream based on the feeling with which you awakened.[3]

Analyze the Characters

The characters you discover in your dreams can be models for your scripts and provide insights through their emotional tone and dream relationships.

ASK

Was I the main character in the dream? Was it my story or did I play a supporting role?

Was I a passive observer or an active participant?

How were my feelings conveyed in the dream? If you felt alienated, you might have been physically separated from everyone else in your dream. If you felt angry, you might have been yelling and screaming at someone. Maybe you wielded a knife or a gun. If you felt ecstatic, you might have been happily flying or skating or sailing or soaring.

How much dialogue was in my dream? What was said? What was conveyed without dialogue?

Did I interact with others in my dream? Was the interaction supportive? Alienating? Conflicting? Was there an antagonist who was determined to keep me from my goal? Did the antagonist succeed or did I barrel through in spite of opposition and conflict?

Was my dream an action-adventure? Did I initiate the action or was I caught up in the action started by someone else? What were the consequences to my action?[4]

Just as real-life experiences are jumping-off points for your work, dreams also can be the beginning of great ideas.

In the following exercise, choose one of your dreams, explore and rework it.

CREATE

Choose a dream. Write a scene exactly as it happened in the dream.

Change the scene by adding more emotions. Make it angrier. More confrontational. More passionate.

Try a new beginning to make it clearer.

Change the ending to make it happier. Create another ending to make it sadder.

Change the actions. Rewrite the scene so that you're the moving force. Rewrite the scene with you as a victim.

Using Your Dreams to Get Inside Characters

Each character in your dreams is a part of you. Choose a dream and put yourself inside each character to understand him or her from the inside out.

Look at the main character in your dream. Describe the person in one or two lines. What do you know about this person? What can you guess about this person's life—where s/he comes from, what s/he's doing, what s/he wants, why s/he's there?

How does this person feel? Does the way you feel change during the course of your dream? If so, how? What are your relationships with others? How are they expressed?

Take two of the characters from your dream and let
them talk to each other. If they fight, let them. See
what kinds of conflicts arise.[5]

Making Every Dream Count

Using the O.N.E. Principle—Observe, Notice, and Experience—look at your dreams in terms of their application to
your specific scripts.

WRITE

Write down the content of your dream.
Write down how you felt during the dream.
Write a scene, using the dream in a script.
Title the dream.

This creative exercise forces a connection between two
unlike ideas—what you found in your dream and how you
might make it usable in a script.

When recording a dream, use present tense to make it
more like a film. Novels are often written in past tense. Films
are watched as if the events are taking place right now.
Here's how this exercise might work with three of my
dreams.

1.

DREAM: I see feet walking through mud.
FEELING: Numbed out. An acceptance of walking through
mud, as if the character explains, "This is what we do."
HOW USED: Possibly prisoners or people from a concen-
tration camp walking through mud and rain.
TITLE: "This Is What We Do" or "Keep Walking."

2.

DREAM: Guido (the character from *Life Is Beautiful*) is
happily and contentedly shaving. Outside, troops are march-
ing. He is unaware that a historical event that will have

terrible consequences is unfolding. His total concentration is on his daily activity.

FEELING: Content, happy, and oblivious.

HOW USED: This could be used as a contrasting scene in many scripts—the character is in his/her own happy world, but something outside, around, nearby is going to threaten this world very soon.

TITLE: "Bad Things Can Take Fools Unaware" or "The Unaware Beware" or "Bad Things Can Come at Any Time."

3.

DREAM: I'm considering not eating dessert, even though the chocolate cake that everyone is carrying looks delicious. I've just about made up my mind when I see that there is also a peach pecan pie for dessert. How could I pass up this original new dessert?

FEELING: Holding my mild frustration: to eat dessert, to not eat dessert?

HOW USED: I'm intrigued by this unusual recipe of peach pecan pie. I'd start exploring the image and imagine what kind of a character would create this recipe. Maybe a great character is lurking in the kitchen.

TITLE: "Choices."

Notice in the above examples, even unusual images are usable. Maybe you dreamt about the fuchsia sofa that sits against the fuchsia walls, maybe you wore a vibrant scarlet dress, maybe you flew with the yellow pig or rode the green elephant.

THINK

Take a vibrant image from one of your dreams and come up with at least ten different ways that you could use it in a film. Since the creative process seeks unlikely combinations, bring together some crazy image from a dream and something already within your script.

YOUR SCRIPT

Do any of your script images come from your dream life? Could any of your dreams inform your script?

Explore the Erotic

The erotic nature of dreams can lead you to creating compelling, powerful, multi-dimensional love scenes. Erotic images are not based on what we *think* is romantic, but on what we *feel* is romantic. The erotic characters in our dreams give us insight into our real-life desires. You never know what lusty guy is going to suddenly show up in your dreams to sweep you away. Who would have thought it was the janitor, or the guy with the scar, or Harvey Keitel?

Not much insight is needed to recognize that most scripts are wish-fulfillment. Many times, women writers write about the ruggedly handsome man who adores the flawed female protagonist. The male screenwriter peoples his script with nubile, beautiful young women who are inflamed with lust for the bookish computer guy. Lots of wishes are put on the page.

Many of these images come from our external life—what our culture and the media has conditioned us to believe is important in the quest for love.

Think about the idealized male and female who have been defined as sexy by Hollywood. The gorgeous blonde bombshell. The dangerous, provocative, highly charged male who is usually insensitive, even bad.

But look to your dream life for your true feelings.

Throughout much of my life, I have had dreams about Gregory Peck. They used to surprise me, and I wondered why he had this hold on my dream life. I thought he was an excellent actor, somewhat attractive (not ruggedly handsome), but I didn't have, or think I had, a "crush" on him. In my dreams, he's a man of great integrity and insight. My image of him is clearly inspired by his role in *To Kill a Mockingbird*. If you asked my conscious mind what kind of a man I would put in a script as a romantic lead, I might produce the ruggedly-handsome-guy stereotype. But my unconscious knows that the men who are most compelling to me are men of integrity—rock-solid, strong in character. This is useful to know when considering whether to date the ruggedly handsome guy or the man of integrity. But it's also useful in creating fictional romantic leads that will grab the hearts of the audience. The man from my dreams has a psychic power. His presence in my dreams tells me what I respect. It clarifies my infatuation with integrity.

Perhaps the male readers of this book have a dream lover who's not attractive or is overweight or is over forty—any qualities that Hollywood has deemed are not sexy. If you only look to Hollywood's stereotypes to tell you what's romantic and sexy, your characters will be one-dimensional, with little emotional resonance. But if you get to know your dream lovers, you will discover these romantic figures come to us unbidden and with strange and soaring power. They can lead you to a great story about the magnificence of a love and to strange and compelling worlds. Chances are, if they have this power to touch you, other people will also respond to them.

Listen to your dreams. They will help you express the truth. If you have the courage to listen to your dreams, you will find characters who can also profoundly touch others.

Dreams and Desires

Our desires and wishes are not just about love and sex, but also about adventures we long to have, and our desire to live life more intensely, more passionately, more fully. Look to your dream adventures to find possibilities for action-adventures and thrillers and mysteries.

LIST

What are some of the desires that have appeared in your dreams? What are those positive, exciting, empowering images that give you insight into what you want and what you could be?

What adventures have you had in your dreams? Have you sailed a ship? Gotten lost in Timbuktu? Been rescued in China? Saved a child?

What abilities have you possessed? Have you shown physical prowess? Great courage? Wisdom and insight? Have you been a photographer? A composer? An intuitive detective or a highly skilled healer?

BRAINSTORM

See if you can come up with a list of at least ten different dream characters or ten different dream stories that have had a profound emotional impact on your dream life.

WRITE

Write out the stories exactly as you remember them.

ANALYZE

Look at what you have. Which one is the most dramatically interesting? What do you think it means? What is it about? Do you have a complete scene? Do you have the beginning of a scene? The middle? The end?

SHARE

If you work with a partner or are in a writing group, you might want to work with each other's dreams—

changing them, combining them, discussing the emotional power of dreams and how you can use them in
your own work.

Remember. Reflect. Make lists. See how much you can
remember of your dream characters through the years.

Getting Answers From Your Dreams

Dreams can present solutions to your screenwriting problems. Define a problem and ask your dreams to give you
an answer. Some writers write out a problem and fold it
under their pillow, waiting for its answer. I also let my
dreams know when I need the information—whether it's
the next morning or in a week. Every time I've done this,
I've discovered the answer when I need it.

One of my favorite writers, Sue Grafton, uses her dreams
to find answers to her writing problems in several ways.
Sometimes she drinks coffee late in the day, knowing that
the caffeine will wake her up in the dead of night. "So I get
to sleep perfectly soundly, and then, at 3:00 A.M., when left
brain is tucked away, not being vigilant, Right Brain comes
out to play and helps me."[6] Sometimes she writes notes to
her more illogical and creative right brain, such as: "Dear
Right Brain, well, sweetie, I've asked you for a little help
with this and I notice you're not forthcoming. I would really
appreciate it if tonight you would solve this problem. Your
pal, Sue." And Sue adds, "And Right Brain, who likes to get
little notes from me, will often come through within a day
or two."[7]

Dreams can help you understand a character from the
inside out. The action in dreams can give you ideas about
ways to keep a story moving or to express a character.

As you collect your dreams, force connections between
them, free-associate, apply all the creative techniques from

Chapter Three—add, subtract, multiply, divide, change the point of view, ask why.

Your dreams and your unconscious mind can deepen your screenplay, but more importantly, deepen you as a person. You will, as a result, be able to bring more insights, emotions, unique images, and original perceptions to your work. However, to achieve an even deeper level to your understanding and your work, you next need to be in touch with your shadow.

8.

Why Your Shadow Is Essential to Your Success as a Writer

What would you like producers to say about your characters?

"What a nice buncha people!"

"Your leading lady is mighty sweet!"

"What a cute character!"

"He's a real pleasant guy to be around!"

Or

"You're a writer with remarkable insights!"

"Your characters spark. They're deep. They're so alive! They're real. They're edgy."

How do you create the unforgettable characters that actors beg to play? That get nominated for Academy Awards? That are worthy of the multi-million-dollar fees demanded by top actors? That might even induce a great actor to do your script for Actor's Guild minimum, because this is the role of a lifetime?

THINK

Who are some of the most memorable film charac-
ters of the last ten or twenty years?

My list would include
Alex (Glen Close) in *Fatal Attraction*,
Stevens (Anthony Hopkins) and Miss Kenton (Emma
    Thompson) in *The Remains of the Day*,
Ripley (Sigourney Weaver) in *Aliens*,
Clarice (Jodie Foster) and Hannibal Lector (Anthony
    Hopkins) in *Silence of the Lambs*,
Bill Munny (Clint Eastwood) in *Unforgiven*,
Sam Gerard (Tommy Lee Jones) in *The Fugitive*.

What do they have in common?

They each have a dark side as well as a light side. You can't
write great characters any other way.

We each contain many contrasting character traits—both
good and bad. Sometimes we're cruel, vindictive, petty, and
hateful. We get jealous of those who are doing well. We want
to kill off our competition. We're greedy and self-centered.
We seek revenge for every hurt and insult. We're insensitive to those in need. We all have our dark side and so
should our characters.

We also have a great capacity for good. We do extraordi-
nary acts of kindness. We're willing to struggle to help each
other, to sit beside each other when sick and dying. We
change the world through our passion for justice, and our
willingness to endure personal sacrifice to gain a greater
good. We can be uncompromising in our integrity. Coura-
geous in our struggle to achieve our ideals. Brave in loving
against all odds. We embrace all these things. So should the
characters we create.

Many great writers are driven by the desire to bring what
is hidden and shadowy into the light and make something

of it—to reveal it, explore it, understand it, transform it. The dark side, the shadow world, is laden with gold—buried treasures that round out a character's personality when used wisely.

If you're unable and unwilling to recognize and articulate human flaws, your characters will be one-dimensional. If you can't see the connection between the shadow and your own life, you write without insight.

This is one of the problems encountered by many of my religious clients. They are well-intentioned people who sincerely want to write films that enrich the human spirit, but they shy away from exposing human flaws or negative characteristics. Their characters have nowhere to go because they start off so nice and perfect. Although these writers want to touch audiences and point the way to hope and resolution, audiences can't identify with perfect characters.

Of course, the opposite is true for many other screenwriters. They are so fascinated by the dark side that they get totally immersed in it. They only write about evil and destruction and manipulation and create characters without light or hope. They love to revel in darkness, presenting images that often become gratuitous and unnatural, decadent, and debased. They too have missed the mark.

Like the too-good images, the too-bad images have no shading nor insight. Both images fail to establish the intrinsic relationship between good and evil. Both fail to acknowledge what psychologists call "the shadow."

What Is the Shadow?

Psychologist Marie Louise von Franz calls the shadow "the dark, unliked, and repressed side."[1] It's the hidden, less-examined, and less-developed part of us that we don't want to admit is there, within us. Poet Robert Bly calls it "the

long bag we drag behind us, heavy with parts of ourselves
our parents or community didn't approve of."[2]

If we are relatively good and decent people, the shadow
contains our dark and destructive side that sometimes surfaces in mean-spirited, malicious, abusive, harmful acts. It
is the forbidden. The taboo. The evil. Most of the time, our
harmful side remains tame and secret, although we're all
quite capable of doing destructive deeds. Sometimes this
side pops out and surprises us—perhaps when we've been
wronged and we lash out. Sometimes it goes beyond a good
tongue-lashing. There are plenty of stories of the sweet,
long-suffering woman who kills her cheating and abusive
husband. Or the quiet boy who tries so hard to follow his
parent's impossible definitions of "being good" that he becomes self-destructive and delinquent.

The dark and even evil part of the shadow is used by
horror writers who dig into their own primordial fears and
the dark caverns of the unconscious. The fears they discover deep within their psyches lead them to create stories that petrify, terrify, horrify. Imagine Stephen King's
shadow! Stephen King acknowledges that all of his horror
stories are based on his dreams. It's clear what kind of
mental and emotional "mining" he's done to write his
novels.

The shadow isn't just evil. It also contains all the scary
things that we don't want to admit are there. John Carpen-
ter defines some of these fears as "death, loss of loved ones,
disfigurement, the unknown."[3] Wes Craven uses his dark
side to "unsettle the audience." He says, "The first maniac
that you have to present to the audience is yourself. You
have to break the taboos and go beyond what anyone thinks
is permissible... And it doesn't have to be gallons of blood
and guts. Sometimes it's the subject matter or a cleverness
of evil, an intelligence to it."[4]

Although the horror film is created from the hidden, frightening—even evil—part of the shadow, the shadow is not just awakened for the making of great horror films. The shadow is more than the ugly and horrible and harmful. It's also the unexpressed, secret, and disowned parts of ourselves that are unacceptable to family, friends, or our culture. They may, or may not, be bad.

Individuals and Cultures Have Their Shadow

As we grew up, our parents, friends, and teachers trained us to be certain kinds of people. They civilized us, acknowledging and affirming certain traits, leading us to suppress their opposites. Perhaps we were defined as "such a pretty little girl" or "such a sweet and happy child" or "isn't he smart?" or "what a great little athlete." Soon, we identified with those explanations, disowning any parts of ourselves that were not sweet and happy, smart and athletic. Sweet and nice qualities received approval, and their opposites were defined as "not good," "evil," "we don't do that in our household." These opposite qualities may have been dark and rebellious, but they may also have been silly, spontaneous, undisciplined, unconventional, nonconformist, or just a bit ugly. Since they weren't allowed, they went underground.

You may think of shadow characteristics as bad, but that depends on who's doing the defining. What's unacceptable can change from family to family or culture to culture. In some families, emotions are bad and being logical is good. These families value a good intellectual discussion, provided it's under control and done with respect. So the emotional side of those family members could be considered "bad" and feelings are hidden.

In other families, everyone shouts and screams and displays their emotions. It's thought of as self-expression. For them, being intellectual and rational might be considered "full of yourself" and not honest, so the thinking side goes underground.

Entire cultures contain shadows. In some cultures, it's good to work long and hard, and any desire to have downtime would be considered lazy and unacceptable. Other cultures consider too much work to be unhealthy. People who are ambitious and have dreams and longings need to hide their desires. Cultures also indoctrinate males and females into what is acceptable. Girls are forced to hide their ambition and love of adventure. Boys never allow anyone to know about their nurturing and gentler sides. The unacceptable hides in the shadow, unexpressed and unintegrated.

When I was in New Zealand, I was told about the "tall poppy syndrome" where equality was accepted, but standing out from the herd was not. Later that same year I went to England, where tall poppies are encouraged, where they receive plaques and awards and monuments, where ambition and achievement are praised and become more important than equality.

Although one might put the Seven Deadly Sins in the shadow, it depends, again, on who's doing the defining. Pride, in U.S. culture, is sometimes considered good, a sign of self-esteem. Humility goes underground. Greed is valued in many capitalist countries, and frugality and simplicity are considered parts of a nutty, impractical Eastern spirituality. If you grew up with a Protestant work ethic, sloth and unemployment and even taking vacations are not allowed. Every culture, religion, and person has a shadow.

If you're a writer who sincerely wants to create quality scripts, working with the shadow will deepen your work. You'll learn how to speak to audiences about struggle and hope and the triumph of the human spirit and the possibility of overcoming one's own darkness and the joy of bringing one's unexpressed good sides into the light. And you'll be able to do it without being cheap and sentimental and easy about it. You'll light a fire under your characters, heat up your drama, and tap into truth.

Start With Yourself

In the following exercises, you'll dredge up shadow material so that you may recognize it, understand it, use it, and transform it. You'll look at dimensions of yourself and your characters, making these dimensions conscious so that you can work responsibly with them as a writer. If your shadow remains unconscious in your writing or in your life, you are in danger of letting it pop out every which way.

Your work with these exercises will be introspective and reflective. You will reach deeply into yourself, acknowledging what's there and integrating it into your writing. However, this is not a psychology book. It is not meant to encourage you to reach into the darkest corners of your life, which can bring on depression. The exercises in this book are merely small stepping stones in your life-long journey toward the self-knowledge that will help you lead a more integrated life and help you write deeper scripts.

The purpose of this book is to help you use the materials of your life and your observations of life—both good and bad—to inform the creation of your characters and to ensure that your writing comes from an honest and authentic place. If you start to feel overwhelmed by any of these exercises, find balance by doing something extroverted— talk to a friend, go for a walk, go to the mall, or play some sports.

You may want to do some of this work with a writing partner or in a trustworthy writing group. If some of the exercises are problematical for you or trigger some difficult memories, you might even want to work with a counselor who can support your journey. This journey can be a rich gold mine or a minefield. I hope it's the former.

REFLECT

Make a list of the qualities that most people would identify as dominant traits in your personality. List these qualities on the left side of the page and list their opposites on the right side. Try to come up with at least twenty to thirty qualities.

My list would include:

DOMINANT	THE OPPOSITE
logical, analytical, rational	emotional/hysterical
well-organized and responsible	flighty and impulsive
happy	sad, morose, depressed
even-tempered	hot-headed
loyal	untrustworthy
generous	miserly
disciplined	spontaneous

Your list of opposites can help you discover your shadow. To what extent do you recognize yourself in this list? Notice, not all of the qualities found among the opposites are fundamentally negative qualities. For example, no one would consider it bad or inappropriate or negative to show sadness when sad things happen. Many people would consider spontaneity and impulsiveness just as important as being responsible and disciplined. This list simply shows that you have qualities that are dominant and affirmed and acceptable, and their opposites, which may be less developed or even hidden.

REFLECT

When have you embraced some of the qualities that appear in your list of opposites? Were you surprised to find yourself behaving like that?

WRITE

Write a scene, based on your own experiences, where you exhibited the oppositional qualities from your list.

THINK

How might you use this experience with a character? Could you see a character doing what you did? Would the character have the same reaction you did?

Triggering the Shadow

Usually our opposite qualities flare up because they're triggered by something. We can triggger or "hook" someone's shadow by reminding them of something embarrassing, shameful, or destructive from their past. As a result, that person might lash out with anger or become depressed. Sometimes our shadows pop out because we're in a relationship with our opposite. His or her dominant traits help bring out our less-developed and hidden side.

In most cases, someone's shadow gets hooked by actions or traits that are diametrically opposed to his or her value system. Suppose that your father is a devout Catholic. He sits in the front pew every Sunday. He's the local priest's best friend. He insisted you go to Catholic school. If you convert to a different religion, you can be sure that your action will hook his shadow.

Suppose that your mother is one of your hometown's most renowned upstanding citizens. She's the head of the P.T.A., president of the Women's Club, and a member of the local chapter of the Daughters of the American Revolution. If you have a baby out of wedlock, you can be sure you'll hook her shadow.

The shadow's response can manifest itself in any number of ways—anger, cattiness, criticism, rejection. It can cause one to be disinherited or kept at the fringes of the family or the fringes of society. Sometimes this response can be volatile, unexpected, and dramatic. These responses make good drama, because they raise the pitch of your story.

ANALYZE

What films show someone's shadow being triggered? Watch several films to see if you can recognize the moment when a character's hidden underside pops out.

A partial list of films to consider might include:

Falling Down	*Batman*	*Hilary and Jackie*
Unforgiven	*Ransom*	*The Apostle*
Death Wish	*It's a Wonderful LIfe*	
A Simple Plan		

THINK

When has your shadow popped out in a particularly dramatic way?

WRITE

Write the scene.

Although I have a stronger intellectual than emotional function, the stress of keeping my emotions hidden has led them to go haywire on more than one occasion, moving me into long crying spells and, on several occasions, into hysterics.

One incident particularly comes to mind. I was a graduate student at Northwestern University, working at the Evanston Children's Theatre at night. One night, at 3:00 a.m., I woke up from a dream, sobbing. The dream was about my friend, Peggy, who worked in the scene shop with me. She was good at her work; I wasn't. During the day she often picked at me for my inability until all my anger came out in the only place it could—my dream life. I had no one to turn to, except Peggy. I called her. She immediately came running over and asked, "What upset you so much?" I told her.

While I projected confidence during the day, my vulnerable shadow was put down and overwhelmed. Although Peggy was usually a caring person, her critical shadow was hooked by my vulnerability.

Any personal incident such as this can serve you well as a writer. You can write about it just as it happened, recognizing that a particular shadow emerged because you (or your character) was not in touch with it. Or you can show a character who knows about their shadow, confronts it, and takes appropriate care of the situation right then and there.

An incident similar to the one above was used for humor in James Brooks' film *Broadcast News.* The efficient, professional, totally competent Jane (Holly Hunter) gets up every morning and sobs for five minutes before going into her control mode.

Psychologists Connie Zweig and Steve Wolf say that we need to romance the shadow to integrate it into our lives. They're not talking about courting evil, but about recognizing that our hidden parts may have value and have something to teach us if we're willing to make friends with them.

I might have romanced my shadow if I had honored my vulnerability and recognized my anger. By valuing my anger (I did have a right to be angry), I might have confronted Peggy over her behavior or been assertive and talked to the head of the scene shop about the problem. Either way might have healed the problem. Both ways have the potential for conflict, drama, and resolution.

This shadow incident can give me insights into other characters who are stressed, hysterical, out of their element, having problems with their friendships, and colliding with someone else's shadow.

You undoubtedly have some shadow experiences in your background. We all do. However, you may find that writing about such an experience is too personal and difficult. If so, write it out, tear it up, write it out again, and tear it up again until you can achieve some level of acceptance of the experience.

The Dastardly Deeds Exercise

In the next few exercises, you will confront some of your shadow characteristics. Familiarize yourself with them, accept them, and integrate them into your writing, recognizing that we're all made up of dark and light. Your characters should be also.

Think about what you consider negative, taboo, or unacceptable. You might also think about what your mother, your minister/priest/rabbi, or your teacher would consider "bad" or "not okay."

THINK

Make a list of the things you were told—either directly or implicitly—not to do.

Here are some possibilities:
Don't be angry.
Don't use that language.
Don't kick grandma.
Don't be noisy.
Don't hit your brother.
Don't be selfish.

REFLECT

Have you ever done these unacceptable, taboo acts? How did you feel after you had done them? Why did they seem so unlike your usual self?

Now dig a little deeper into your shadow.

THINK

List the five or ten most wild, daring, crazy, shocking, embarrassing, uncharacteristic actions you've done or considered doing.

Here are some shocking possibilities. If you haven't done them, have you ever thought of doing them?

REMEMBER

Have you ever shoplifted?
Cross-dressed?
Skinny-dipped?
Gone to a nudist camp?
Have you ever slept with a priest or nun?
Done an illegal act, didn't get caught, and were glad you did it anyway?
Plotted or planned a murder, even if only in a passing fantasy?

If you feel horror, embarrassment, fear, shame, guilt, and trepidation as you remember them, that's fine. Breathe, and relish the feeling. If you can get an emotional charge out of these thoughts, great. You aren't going to act them out. But some great characters have undoubtedly done these acts. If you can find these characters in yourself, you are more capable of writing them.

WRITE

How could you use such actions in a scene? What types of characters might have done similar things? Write about a character who shoplifts or skinny-dips or commits some illegal act. Capture both the character's actions and the character's emotions. Try to express the value system that these actions challenge.

ANALYZE

What films have characters doing crazy, shocking, daring, or embarrassing deeds?

A partial list might include:

Natural Born Killers	*Strangers on a Train*
Bonnie and Clyde	*The Butcher Boy*
The River Wild	*Shadow of a Doubt*
Life Is Beautiful	*River's Edge*
Deliverance	*Pulp Fiction*
Dog Day Afternoon	*There's Something About*
Touch of Evil	*Mary*
Fatal Attraction	*The Godfather*
Silence of the Lambs	*Apocalypse Now*

Getting Stuck in the Shadow

Some of these films not only show characters acting out their shadows, but they show characters stuck in the shadows. Some, like *Bonnie and Clyde*, revel in the darkness. They love the daring shadow life. Some, like *Fatal Attraction*, show a character in the grip of the shadow, but with no skills to move from the shadow into the light. In *Fatal Attraction*, Alex knows she's unhappy, but she projects her shadow onto Dan, who she believes isn't doing right by her. Some, like the characters in *Pulp Fiction*, seem oblivious to the shadow's hold on their lives.

Some characters are unable to escape their evil, rebellious, harmful shadows. They're unable to transform darkness into light. However, an audience watching such characters on the screen might find itself warned, instructed, and transformed by the dire consequences that befall these characters.

Generating Emotional Heat

In most films, transformation occurs. Characters move from the shadow into the light. Emotions are the heat generated as the shadows emerge. Many films seem unemotional because there is no movement and therefore no energy.

ANALYZE

Go back to your list of dastardly deeds that you did in your past. Did any contain violent, unacceptable emotions?

Reflect on your own emotional sparks.

REMEMBER

Have you ever been so angry you hurt someone?
Have you ever been insanely jealous?
Have you ever had unbridled sexual urges?
Have you ever had lust in your heart?
Have you ever taken revenge on someone or wanted to?
Have you ever been so afraid that you thought there was no way out?

WRITE

Write the scene *exactly* as it happened.

DEFINE

Give a title to the scene that defines the shadow (i.e., A Lusty Day or Anger Is Outed, etc.)

ANALYZE

Look at the scene. Did you get it down as it happened with its full emotional range?

RE-SHAPE

Is the shadow clear in your scene? Is it as emotional and as dramatic as it could be? If not, re-shape the scene to express the shadow. To do this, you might add, subtract, re-form, re-structure, or even change the characters. Can you re-shape the scene so it's more powerful? More violent? More dramatic? More confrontational? More despairing? More frustrating? More embarrassing? More shameful?

Notice how much emotional energy—high drama—comes out of your shadow. As you look at these characteristics (shadow qualities) that you might want to get rid of, or certainly not tell anyone about, recognize that they are part of you. They may not be the biggest part of you and may not be the best part of you, but they are usable. If you, as a multi-dimensional person, have these characteristics, then your characters should have them also.

What Happens to the Shadow?

To repress parts of ourselves forever is difficult. Eventually, the shadow demands to be heard. When first it rears its head, we might be frightened and wonder, "Who was that? It couldn't be me—I'm nice."

If our shadow qualities don't have a chance to be a part of our personalities, we can get petrified into an image of ourselves. If your parents always told you to "be nice," your feelings of anger and jealousy and hurt and sadness would go underground, festering. It's then easy to become frozen into a persona—to become a kind of Stepford wife who can't show any other side of herself and has no compassion for anyone except other sweet and happy people.

The shadow is recognizable throughout every part of our culture. Notice how often a serial killer has been defined as "such a nice, quiet young man." Priests and ministers preach against sex in the pulpit and are in the headlines the next week for molesting young boys, visiting prostitutes, and groping flight attendants. Nice, religious girls have babies out of wedlock. The stable family man commits suicide when unemployed or bankrupt. Notice how many self-righteous people have been found to have more than a few skeletons in their closets. The shadow is alive and well in every corner of our lives.

Getting It Into the Light

Sometimes the shadow is healthy and vital. You've certainly heard stories about the abused housewife who goes back to school, divorces her husband, and starts to enjoy a fulfilling and dynamic lifestyle. Or the person who's been put down by his parents all his life, goes into therapy, and there lets out his very confident and competent shadow, allowing him to become a successful professional.

Usually a person is transformed because some part of his or her shadow that is positive and good surfaces and is integrated into his or her personality. The person becomes healed of their past and becomes a deeper, more whole person.

Some of the greatest films have looked at the transformation from the ugly and bad and dark into the good, the light, the redemptive. But how does one make this transition? Not by talking about it. Not by one character telling another to "Be Good." This transition is made through resistance, obstacles, and emotions that keeping pushing a character back and forth from darkness to light.

You can understand this concept by thinking of your own difficult transformations that came not from repressing your negative side, but by redeeming it.

How is this done?

When I wrote *When Women Call The Shots*, I was surprised that some readers found my ideas controversial. I wondered why anyone would have trouble with a book that affirmed women's gifts and their importance to the film industry. Because I consider myself a diplomatic, non-confrontational, non-political, non-combative person, when I hit this resistance, I got scared. I wanted to retreat, to tone down my comments, to not take a stand, to be more careful, to go back into my sweet and light side where everyone agreed with me. One of my friends laughed about my response and clarified that "any book about women is controversial. Accept it!" She helped me see that I could have an important influence on women's struggle for equality in the workplace by being willing to take a stand. I could still be diplomatic, but strong. I could still be non-confrontational, but truthful.

My activist side, which was part of my shadow, was pushed out by my greater desire for justice and equality. My sweet and nice side wanted to keep pushing it back because I thought it "wasn't me" and "wasn't acceptable." Through the support of friends and other readers who were touched and changed by the book, I could make friends with my shadow. I could allow a transformation toward integrity.

The transformation from shadow to light usually hits a snag. There's a glitch, an inner conflict. We want to play it safe and stay with what's familiar. Yet, some sense of integrity is pulling us toward speaking up for what we believe. We feel a push-pull and don't know which to choose. Change sometimes demands a sacrifice—a sacrifice of a relationship or a change in how we understand ourselves. We become vulnerable when we venture out into new territory. Yet, if we don't, we feel as if we are not developing some important part of ourselves.

REFLECT

What transformations have you made in your own life?
Were you defensive, but now you're more open?
Were you impatient, but now you're patient?
Were you scared, but now you're confident?
Were you short-tempered, but now you've learned to express your emotions without flying off the handle?

QUESTION

Who helped you transform?

A teacher?   Your spouse?
A friend?   Your children?
A lover?   A religious leader?
A therapist?

QUESTION

How did s/he help?

Through confrontation?   Through caring?
Through example?   Through self-sacrifice?
Through threats?   Through encouragement?

THINK

What obstacles and conflicts might keep you (or the characters you're creating) from making a transformation from shadow to light?

MAYBE IT'S
fear
shyness

lack of confidence
uncertainty
insecurity
inertia

WRITE

Write a scene showing a transformation of your
shadow from dark to light.

As you write the scene, show your transformational arc as
you progress from darkness to light. The hidden, shadowy
aspect of your character emerges, has an emotional reaction, confronts resistance, and finally moves victoriously
into the light.

Transforming the Shadow

Up to this time, I've emphasized being in touch with the
shadow. But if the shadow is going to be transformed, you
also need to be in touch with The Good.

REMEMBER THE GOOD

When have you been so ecstatic you felt you were
glowing?
When have you cared deeply for another person or a
cause?
When have you courageously stood up for the right?
When have you bravely overcome limitations?
When have you accomplished a great feat?

ANALYZE

What did The Good look like? In what dramatic,
active images was The Good manifested?

List some films that show goodness as dramatic,
emotional, and complex.

My list would include:

Dead Man Walking. Nothing sweet and simpering and easy about Sister Helen Prejean (Susan Sarandon).

One True Thing. Ellen Gulden (Renée Zellweger) found her goodness through honesty, intuition, and sacrifice, and developed a stronger relationship with her mother and her father as a result.

Sense and Sensibility. Elinor Dashwood (Emma Thompson) struggled with her feelings of jealousy versus integrity, which eventually brought her the love of Edward.

Look to your own experiences to know what transformation feels like and how the journey from un-transformed to transformed is accomplished. Then apply what you've learned to your characters. Do you want your character to be happier? More joyful? Do you want your characters to care more? To commit? Use your experiences and emotions to help you get it on the page.

Finding Shadow Transformations in Films

To understand how this transformation works in films, look at some that give us glimpses into the shadow as characters move through their conflicts and confusion and struggles into the light.

THINK

Make a list of films in which the main character has been flawed and you've seen evidence of the shadow. Think of a scene that reveals his or her shadow characteristics and scenes that show the transformation.

Dead Man Walking. Notice how Mathew Poncelet (Sean Penn) found redemption by moving past denial into confession. It wasn't enough to read the Bible. He had to do something! It's the difficulty of the journey and the depth of his evil that makes this a great film.

A Christmas Carol. Why has the story of Scrooge endured for so long? Because his mean-spiritedness was transformed through much resistance until his heart was softened.

An Officer and a Gentleman. Zack Mayo (Richard Gere), desensitized by his past, was unable to enter into intimate personal relationships. In the face of great personal resistance, he learned to love.

ANALYZE

What are your favorite films about transformation? What do you love about them? Why? What were their transformations? In what ways do you identify with these transformations? How did you feel after you saw these films? Have you ever seen a film that caused you to undergo changes in your life?

Some of my favorite transformation films include:

It's a Wonderful Life	*Working Girl*
Dead Poets Society	*Awakenings*
Thelma & Louise	*Good Will Hunting*
Schindler's List	

Accepting the Valuable Shadow World

Some films show the shadow world as valuable and unconventional and the commonly acceptable world as inhibiting and repressive. Think about what films might show the positive shadow.

My list would include:

The Truman Show. Truman moves his shadow (the desire for freedom) into light through becoming reflective, spontaneous, confused, crazy, and determined.

Titanic. Rose was inhibited by the conventions of her day, but her shadow side was daring and unconventional. Through her love for Jack, she found an inner freedom and a way to create a life of value.

Norma Rae. It was acceptable for Norma to follow the rules and be a good worker. Her hidden side was her passion for justice. First with uncertainty and then with assertiveness, she moved from shadow into light.

Schindler's List. Schindler's goodness was his shadow, which was hidden to him. He was ambivalent about his goodness until the end. (Look at the One-Armed Man scene, where Schindler has trouble being kind.)

The Horse Whisperer. Annie defined herself in terms of her professional success and business acumen. By remaining in Montana long enough, she discovered the hidden quiet lover of nature within her. She met her shadow, and it brought her balance. (Look at the horseback-riding scene in which Annie's hidden side comes out and heals her.)

STUDY

Take one film from your list and watch it. Find scenes that portray that character's flaws, goodness, and transformative moments.

WRITE

Write one scene exactly as it's shown in the film.

CREATE

Pretend you've been asked to rewrite the script. You've been hired to add two new shadow scenes to further dimensionalize the character. Write them.

YOUR SCRIPT

Have you brought out the shadow in your script? Is it transformed and integrated? Have you clearly

defined the shadow, the light, and the snags
the characters encounter on their ways to
transformation?

Moving Beyond Black and White

One can't be creative without the flexibility that comes
from seeing one possibility, and then seeing its opposite. If
a writer is afraid of the shadow, s/he'll always be censor-
ing, saying, "I would never write about that." If censorship
comes too early in the process, you can't get to the heart
of the matter.

Some writers are afraid that if they examine their
shadow, they'll lose their creativity. In fact, shadow work
will enhance your creativity by expanding your ability to
work with ambivalence and opposition.

Adding flaws to your characters humanizes them. Audiences identify with imperfect characters who are like them.
Through your understanding of the shadow, your characters can become real, truthful, and unforgettable.

9.

Creating Dynamic Characters
Through Opposition

Great writers love conflict. They love the drama, the spark, the sizzle, the spice that comes from a dramatic clash between two characters with two opposing goals.

Other writers shy away from it. They want to play nice, to have their characters all get along, not to make waves.

If you're afraid of conflict, your characters will be flat and bland. Why? Because great characters are built on the concept of opposition.

There's opposition between the antagonist and protagonist.

In great dialogue, there's opposition between text and subtext—what a character says and what a character really means.

There is opposition between what characters want and yearn for and what stands in the way of them getting it—whether it's outer obstacles or inner fear.

Great character relationships are built on contrasts—qualities of one character that are opposite to another.

Characters are usually transformed by their opposites.

There is opposition between a character's light and dark sides, the outer persona and the shadow.

There's opposition between the evil and the good within the villain. Even Good can be ambivalent. Nothing is simple in human life.

Using Janusian Thinking

Another word for oppositional thinking is Janusian thinking (from the Roman god Janus, who is usually depicted with two faces). This is defined by creativity researcher Albert Rothenberg as "conceiving two or more opposite or seemingly contradictory ideas, images, or concepts simultaneously."[1]

When you first read this definition, it might sound strange or nonsensical. But in the context of the multi-dimensionality of film, a great screenwriter is always creating multiple images, ideas, stories, and characters that are all going to happen on screen at the same time.

If you can't consider a multitude of possibilities when writing and rewriting a script, your creativity will be limited.

This chapter will build on the visual thinking you learned in Chapter Six and on the work you did with the shadow in Chapter Eight. It will progress from working with oppositional thinking in scenes to oppositional thinking as it applies to characters.

REMEMBER

What are the most visually arresting films you've seen? *The Last Emperor? Seven Years in Tibet? Barry Lyndon? Lawrence of Arabia? Saving Private Ryan? The Thin Red Line?*

VISUALIZE

Imagine a scene from one of these films. Think about that scenes' visual images. Notice what's in the foreground and what's in the background.

You might imagine the scene where the small boy-emperor in *The Last Emperor* comes through the yellow-orange curtain to greet his thousands of bowing subjects. Notice the opposition in the scene—small versus large, one versus the masses, vulnerable child versus the attitude of the subjects who see him as invulnerable and all-powerful.

You might think of some scenes in *The Thin Red Line* in which writer-director Terence Malick contrasted the blood and horror and mayhem of war with the quiet, serene beauty of nature.

In *Wall Street*, Gekko works out financial deals that cause havoc in everyone's life, while in the background his child plays.

You may want to watch *Life Is Beautiful* to see the humor in one part of the frame, the seriousness in another.

Many of David Zucker's films work with foreground and background opposition. In *Naked Gun 2½*, Frank Drebbin (Leslie Nielsen) comes out of the men's room and unwittingly slams the door into Barbara Bush's face. She continues to stagger around in the background as he continues to be oblivious.

Later, Drebbin talks to Ed (George Kennedy) as they're served drinks. As the waiter turns around, we see his bare backside.

In *Ruthless People* (written by Dale Launer, directed by David Zucker), Danny De Vito is visited by the police. In the background, two cops play tennis.

IMAGINE

Imagine a scene from a horror film in which high-school kids celebrate in the foreground, because they think the monster is dead, but in the background, we see the monster at the window.

Imagine the proud mountaineer coming to the top of the mountain, and behind him his partner is falling off.

Imagine the woman in jeopardy who thinks that she's safe, but behind her the door opens slowly.

Imagine a scene at a country manor where everyone celebrates the end of the harvest. Behind the house, the barn is on fire.

Make up a scene, imagining the foreground of the scene as serious while something very silly or horrible or unexpected happens in the background.

If you can imagine these scenes in your mind, you've begun to practice oppositional thinking. Notice how contrasting realities add tension and conflict and suspense to a scene.

YOUR SCRIPT

Is there any scene in your script where there's opposition between the foreground and background? If not, could there be?

Janusian thinking forces your mind into creative patterns. As you hold two diametrically opposed ideas in your mind at the same time, your mind is forced to become more flexible because you're thinking of one idea, its opposite, and everything in between.

Practicing Simultaneous Thinking

Two different aspects comprise Janusian thinking. One is simultaneous thinking—focusing on two ideas or images at the same time. The other is oppositional thinking—considering two ideas that are opposed to one another.

In the following exercises, you'll practice the movement from sequential (cause-and-effect) thinking to simultaneous thinking. After some practice with simultaneous thinking, we'll make it more complex by working with oppositional thinking.

Imagine the following scenes sequentially.

Imagine a suave-looking character, drinking at a high-falutin' cocktail party. If you want to imagine James Bond, go ahead.

Next, imagine the same character drinking the last drops of soy milk, while standing next to a garbage can behind a natural-foods store, surrounded by kind shoppers giving him change, even though he never asked for it.

Using Janusian thinking, imagine the two images on screen at the same time.

You might notice that, in trying to see these two images simultaneously, your mind went through a process of some sort. Which of the following did you automatically do?

1. You see the images shift back and forth.

2. You see the image as a split screen.

3. You see one image at the top of the screen and pan down to the other image at the bottom.

4. You see one image in the foreground and the other in the background, so they occupy different spaces within the frame.

5. You superimpose one image on top of the other, as if you caught the image in a dissolve.

6. You blend the images together, morphing them, taking some qualities from one image and some qualities from the other and creating a new image.

Technically, Janusian thinking would be the ability to think simultaneously, as in Numbers 2, 4, and 5. But all six of these images might be used in a script you write. Practice until you can hold both images on the screen at the same time.

ANALYZE

Which of these six images are the most dramatically interesting?

If this is difficult (and it well may be—it's advanced visual thinking), either keep practicing or go back to the visualization exercises in the sensation chapter, work on them some more, and then return to this chapter.

Think of five to ten other scenes that could fall under the heading "character drinking."

Notice, by allowing your mind to consider alternatives, you've freed your mind from being stuck in the obvious. You've taken away the limits to your thinking. You've allowed your mind to move outside sequential time into creative time. You've discovered that you can consider alternatives at the same time, rather than having to look at them one at a time.

In order to further train your mind in Janusian thinking, here are some images to play with.

Imagine a character ready to commit a crime. He takes up a gun. He takes up a knife. Imagine five other weapons. Can you hold several possible weapons in your mind at once? Think through the consequences of these choices.

Complicate this exercise.

Once you imagine five different weapons, imagine how a character would commit a crime using all of them. What if your character has a rifle under his arm, a knife in his left hand, a club in his right, a bomb laced to his back, and knives protruding from his boots? What kind of a crime do you see this character committing?

YOUR SCRIPT

Look at the actions and choices your characters make. Consider their opposites. Change your characters' gender or race. See what's more dramatically interesting. Might some opposing actions take place simultaneously?

Creativity researcher Albert Rothenberg says that the ability to think oppositionally is so important that it's a key defining characteristic of the creative mind.

Have you ever experienced ideas coming to you so quickly that you can't write them down fast enough? You think of one idea and its opposite and everything in between. Your mind is in a non-linear time zone. It's creative time.

When our minds are flexible, we think in layers that contain many possibilities—AND/OR, YES/NO, and MAYBE/MAYBE NOT. We don't think on a one-dimensional plane; we focus on the tensions between and within characters and images and themes, juggling all the different script elements at the same time.

Creating Characters Through Oppositional Thinking

The ability to incorporate opposite qualities without being schizophrenic is one of the marks of the creative personality as well as the great character.

Just as creative artists must maintain and juggle opposing thoughts and desires and traits, so must great characters.

Below is a list of opposing traits and some films that contain characters who are built on these oppositional elements. Can you add other films to this list?

Aggression and cooperation (*Shogun*)
Wisdom and foolishness (*Life Is Beautiful, King Lear*)
Playfulness and discipline (*Patch Adams*)
Responsibility and irresponsibility (*Big*)
Fantasy and reality (*Kramer vs. Kramer*)
Extroversion and introversion (*Shine, Surviving Picasso*)
Introspection and social action (*Gandhi*)
Humility and pride (*Braveheart*)
Self-concern and selflessness (*Missing, It's a Wonderful Life*)
Aggression and nurture (*The Terminator*)
Domination and submission (*Pulp Fiction*)
Sensitivity and rigidity (*Hercule Poirot* and *Sherlock Holmes*)
Masculinity and femininity (*Alien, The Terminator*)[2]

ANALYZE

Look back at this list of films. Analyze how their oppositional tensions dramatically propel their characters.

REFLECT

Although it might make you a bit crazy, imagine all these opposing qualities as parts of your own personality.

If you're in touch with your own oppositional qualities, your writing will be real and true. Your heroes and villains will be authentic. Your portrayals of people of the opposite sex and people from other cultures will be authentic.

Your characters will have more personality layers, more humanity.

REFLECT

Think of your favorite action-adventure films— perhaps *Die Hard* or *The Fugitive* or *Raiders of the Lost Ark.* Imagine the lead played by a woman. How might the gender change affect the character? How might it make the character more interesting?

Think of your favorite female-driven relationship drama, whether it's *Fried Green Tomatoes* or *Steel Magnolias* or *Hilary and Jackie* or *Enchanted April.* Imagine the lead(s) being played by a man. How would changing gender affect the story?

Can you imagine these characters as having an-drogynous characteristics without the men being wimps and the women being too tough?

Yearnings

In any dramatic writing, your protagonist has a desire, want, an intention, a goal. That's what drives the character and the story. Something stands in opposition to what the character wants or there's no story. What is this resistance? Why is the goal so difficult to achieve?

To get at the answer, begin with yourself. Think of what you want, what you yearn for, and what stands in opposition to your desires.

For the last ten years, I've been fascinated by the idea of yearning. We often lose our passions and yearnings as we grow older. We stop following a dream, saving money to go on that romantic vacation, actively searching for true love or a new place to call home. Our yearnings diminish to a simple "like to": "I'd like to go to Europe some day."

"Maybe, I'd like to get one of those cars next year." There's a bit of a yawn to a "like to." It's idle conversation, not a driving force.

A "have to" can be a driving force. But "have to" often comes from others, not from within ourselves. "You gotta get a job or you'll be tossed out of this house." "You have to find the bad guy or the world will blow up."

But nobody tells us what we're supposed to yearn for. Yearnings push and pull at us. We feel yearnings throughout the body. Yearnings are sometimes so powerful that they're secret. We want them so badly that we don't want to dissipate their energy by talking about them to just anyone. Sometimes they're so strange that we wonder what anyone would think about us if they really knew what we yearned for, or how much we yearned for it.

Too many characters lack guts and vibrancy because they only have a wee bit of want, rather than raging desires. To create more energetic characters, deeper characters, give them a driving force and a yearning.

REFLECT

What do you yearn for? To visit a certain culture? To have a home in the country? To sell a script? To be loved and cherished by a spouse? Perhaps to cuddle and care for a child?

ANALYZE

What do your yearnings have in common? Do they follow a theme of success? A desire for freedom? For fulfillment? To get away?

The opposition that keeps us from achieving the goals we yearn for often comes from within ourselves.

REFLECT

What inner resistance gets in the way of making your goals happen? Where is the push-pull, the "I want it, "the "I don't want it"?

Do you feel a fight within yourself between intimacy and freedom? You say you want a relationship, but on some level you must not want it.

Do you feel a conflict between the desire for the stability that comes from children and the desire not to be tied down?

Do you have a fear of success or a conflict between a desire to be rich and famous and the fear that if you are, you'll lose all your friends?

Do you have a place you want to visit, but you're afraid that if you go there, you may be out of your element?

Do you have a passion for some kind of social action, but think that if you follow through with it, some people won't like you?

Do you have a desire to learn a new skill, but think you're too old or not capable enough to learn it?

People often sabotage the achievement of their goals by failing to value the yearnings that push them toward getting what they want. They acquiesce to the inner fears that resist change.

But our obstacles are not just from within ourselves. They also come from the antagonists in our lives who just don't want us to achieve our souls' desires.

THINK

Who opposes your yearning, whether it's to sell a script or to marry the guy you're in love with or to go away for three weeks to a Greek Island? What outer obstacles stand in your way? How do family, teachers, institutions, friends, and neighbors try to stop you?

REFLECT

How do you get around them or through them? Or do you? How do you deal with the conflicts in these situations?
Do you confront resistance head-on?
Give in to it?
Clarify your yearning and recognize your resistance to it. Be specific.

WRITE

Write a scene in which you yearn for something and achieved it, in spite of obstacles. Show the yearning. Show the resistance. Show the achievement of the goal.

ANALYZE

Think of some films that deal with yearnings. What do you learn about yearnings from these films?

Here's part of my list:

Shirley Valentine/Enchanted April show the yearning for freedom and beauty and identity that is opposed by society's conventional concepts of marriage.

Shakespeare in Love/The Karate Kid/Shine/Flashdance/ Rocky/My Fair Lady/Roman Holiday show a yearning to actualize a part of one's self. Some of the oppositional forces include respectable society, competition from others, and an inner vulnerability within the protagonist.

Not Without My Daughter/Escape From Alcatraz/The Shawshank Redemption show the yearning for freedom, the opposition of a social context, and the question of "Whom do I trust?"

Don't forget social yearnings—the yearnings for justice, (*Gandhi, The Verdict, Norma Rae, Mississippi Burning*), for equality (*Cry Freedom*), for education (*Educating Rita, Lean on Me, Stand and Deliver*), to better one's self (*She-Devil, Living Out Loud, Unmarried Woman*), to preserve the environment (*Fly Away Home*), to be free (*Amistad*).

WRITE

Think of a film about yearnings. (You can use one of the ones listed above). Imagine that you've been hired to rewrite this film, and you've been asked to add two more scenes that clarify the push-pull between yearning and fear. Can you create the scenes, using opposition between the foreground and background, opposition within the character, and conflict between protagonist and antagonist?

YOUR SCRIPT

What does your character yearn for? What's the oppositional force working against him/her?

Notice, characters start to gain dignity and integrity when they take their yearnings seriously. Notice how they gain hope and strength. Notice how the audience roots for them.

Finding the Conflict

Most people are uncomfortable with conflict in their own lives. They move away from it, don't want to talk about it, sweep it under the rug. But conflict gives life to drama, and the screenwriter needs to learn how to confront, build, and resolve conflict.

Conflict depends on oppositional thinking. What do you oppose? What do you dislike? What do you reject? In most conflict situations, two people want opposite and exclusive goals. One will win. One will lose.

Conflict ignites emotions—anger, rage, frustration, hurt feelings, feeling belittled and betrayed, put down and insulted. These emotions, once ignited, might find themselves expressed through shouting, blowing up the world, or punching someone in the nose.

Although we often avoid conflict in real life, in drama we move toward it. To write great dramas, you must tune into conflict, which you'll discover is all around you.

ACT

Go through a day and tune in to the potential conflicts that are around you. What are their possibilities? Did the dry cleaner forget a spot? You could have yelled about it, but instead you covered the spot with jewelry. Did the deli clerk slop on too much mayonnaise? You could have made an issue of it, but it didn't seem to matter. When your parents belittled you or didn't understand what you were doing, did you say something and start an argument or a discussion, or did you just take it and feel small? Did a wildly careening driver cut you off on the freeway? Did someone reject your script? Did you fail to receive a deserved promotion? If so, how did you respond to these conflicts?

Notice all the ways that conflict is avoided, confronted, or resolved.

ANALYZE

What are your favorite conflict scenes in films? Analyze these conflicts. Are they conflicts over a value system? An attitude? What action to take? Between the powerful and the powerless?

WRITE

Using one of the films you analyzed above as a model, write a new scene that contains the same kind of conflict.

Although most conflicts in drama are expressed as win/ lose situations, they don't have to be. Some films express win/win resolutions to conflict. Here are a few of my favorite win/win conflict scenes:

Howard's End. Henry (Anthony Hopkins) breaks his engagement when his fiancée, Margaret (Emma Thompson), discovers he had an affair with Jackie. Margaret lovingly confronts him and forgives him.

To Kill a Mockingbird. The mob is ready to lynch Tom when the little girl, Scout, defuses the situation by humanizing it.

Strictly Ballroom. The father is not happy that his daughter is dancing with the boy. He confronts him— "You dance the Pasodoble? Show me!" The conflict is dissipated as the father and grandmother teach the boy to dance from his heart.

YOUR SCRIPT

Is conflict in every scene in your script? Between which characters? How is it acted out? Have you explored all the potential conflicts, or are your characters (and you) shying away from them? Push the conflict. Give your characters stronger opinions. Give them more confrontations. Try creating a fight. Is your script dramatically stronger now?

Getting to Know the Antagonist

Using oppositional thinking, explore the antagonist in your story. The antagonist is the opposing force. S/he may be a villain (the bad guy who wants to do you harm) or the person who stands in your way: the customs officer who can't let you through because you don't have the proper passport, the teacher who gave you that well-deserved B that kept you from getting into Harvard, the parents who said they didn't have money for ballet lessons.

Even villains are not simple and one-dimensional. None of us has known a totally evil person. Look deeply. Even the bad guy has yearnings (and usually an unhappy child-hood). Although we may not have known really evil people, all of us have known people who are mean-spirited, malicious, manipulative, ego-driven, selfish, self-involved, insensitive, harsh, and abusive.

To create an antagonist, you must possess some understanding of human nature. If you draw this character from your dreams and life experiences, audiences will feel and respond to the powerful ambiguity of this character's very human evil.

Great villains are based on opposition. While the story may focus on their evil traits, the great writer will also shade in the good. Think of the scenes in *The Godfather* where the godfather is watching the baptism of his grandson while his men follow his orders, killing his enemies. In *Wall Street*, Gordon Gekko seems particularly attentive to his infant son. In many James Bond films, the villain loves his cat or his fish or takes good care of his workers.

What is villainy? We're so used to seeing movie villains as one-dimensional people ready to blow up the world or manipulate the financial markets that we get a very limited view of evil. Real life is much more complex. And in great films, there are deep insights into the nature of evil.

REFLECT

How do you see evil? What are evil intentions? What are evil deeds?

I see evil as harmful acts that constrict, oppress, limit, control, and manipulate. They're the acts that keep someone from expressing his or her true gifts. That limit his or her humanity. That stop the good work of creating, nurturing, loving, caring. These include the Seven Deadly Sins of Pride, Sloth, Lust, Envy, Gluttony, Covetousness, and Anger as well as all the harm that is done through irresponsibility, dishonesty, and insensitivity.

REFLECT

What other sins, evil actions, harmful acts would you put on your list? What harm do they do?

REMEMBER

What people have you met whom you consider negative? Harmful? Abusive? Jot down some of the actions they've done, some of the attitudes that they've expressed.

Don't just work with the big negative actions that you read about in the newspaper. Look at the smaller harmful acts that, over a period of time, can add up to a life of abuse and loss of self-esteem. Think about some of the great villains, such as Iago from *Othello*, whose harmful acts were based on insinuations, murmurings, and suggestions.

How does oppositional thinking work within the villain?

It's clear that your villain opposes your protagonist and opposes the good. But a great villain also has inner ambivalence—the opposite qualities that make the evil more insidious because it's colored by shades of goodness.

THINK

As you remember the abusive and harmful people you've met in your own life, make a list of their negative qualities and of their good qualities.

Here's a list based on some of the people that I've met.

NEGATIVE	POSITIVE
Manipulative	Competent, Efficient
Picky	Could be funny
Secretive	Insightful
Controlling	Very smart
Manipulative with workers	Loves children
Selfish	Hard-working
Angry/Enraged	Artistic and musical
Dishonest	Faithful to his wife
Intolerant/Racist	Loves his family

CREATE

Create a one- to four-page scene that shows a negative quality in action. How does this action affect the other characters in the scene? Did the action diminish another person, thereby affecting his/her self-esteem? Did it physically hurt another person? Did it confuse, anger, or insult another person? Show the relationship between the action and another character's response to the action.

YOUR SCRIPT

What good qualities does your antagonist have? Have you shaded them into his or her character?

Just as the evil can include the good, so do good people include such negative qualities as selfishness, insensitivity, defensiveness, intolerance, low self-esteem, and unreliability.

Portraying good but dimensional characters in films is difficult. Either the character is so good that we can't identify with him or her, or the flaws take over and there are few moments of compassion and care and integrity—or whatever qualities we can consider to be of greatest value.

ANALYZE

Look at films that show the ambivalence of goodness. Some of these films include: *The Remains of the Day*, *Silence of the Lambs*, *Thelma & Louise*, *Casablanca*, *The Shawshank Redemption*, *Beauty and the Beast*, *The Crying Game*.

The film *Schindler's List* stands out as a superb example of the ambivalence of the good. When Schindler (Liam Nielson) asks Stern (Ben Kingsley) to draw up a list of his factory workers whom he's going to relocate, Stern asks:

> STERN
> What did Goeth say about this? You just told him how many people you needed and—
>
> (pause)
>
> You're not buying them?

> SCHINDLER
> If you're still working for me, I'd expect you to talk me out of it—it's costing me a fortune!

Later, when Schindler wants to add Goeth's maid to the list, Goeth seems to show the smallest inclination of a tender heart until we realize the horror of his perverted value system.

GOETH
It wouldn't be right...The most merciful thing I could
do would be to take her into the woods and shoot her
painlessly in the back of the head.[3]

Creating Transformations Through Opposition

The most dramatic relationships in our lives are transformative. The people who have an impact on us can break
us down or make us grow. People give us advice. If it's good
and if we take it, it helps us for the better. Sometimes we're
mentored or affirmed by authority figures. Sometimes we
get a lucky break and stretch our abilities to live up to our
potential. Sometimes we're forced to change because if we
don't change, we'll lose everything that's valuable to us.

Usually the people with the greatest impact on our lives
are our opposites. They know what we don't know. They
have abilities we wish we had. They aren't hooked by those
things that hook us, so they can see our struggles clearly.
They act in ways that we admire but aren't yet part of our
repertoire.

REFLECT

What have been your transformations in life? Who
helped you achieve them? What was the force that
wanted you to stay where you were? What was the
opposing force that pushed you to change? What
were the story beats that moved you from being one
kind of person to being another kind of person? Did
you have to become transformed to be committed
to a marriage partner? To get a job? To have better
friends?

ANALYZE

Choose a film with a strong transformational arc.
Re-watch the film, writing down every story beat,
every event, every character action and response
that led to the transformation of the protagonist.
Some of these moments will be expressions of that
character's shadow. Others will come out through
dialogue, yearnings, and conflicts that get
transcended.

Here are some films that you might want to watch:

Wall Street	*Awakenings*
The Piano	*Good Will Hunting*
Working Girl	*Ryan's Daughter*
Elizabeth	*The Fisher King*
The Verdict	*Schindler's List*
Fly Away Home	*Ordinary People*
Charley	*An Unmarried Woman*
The Miracle Worker	*Tootsie*
The Secret Garden	*The African Queen*
Starting Over	*A Civil Action*
Muriel's Wedding	*It's a Wonderful Life*
Kramer vs. Kramer	*Private Benjamin*

YOUR SCRIPT

Analyze and reflect on the transformational arc in
your own script. Are the beats clear? Are they
expressed more through action than through
dialogue?

Double Lives

Have you ever been intrigued by the idea of living a parallel
life or a double life? Or cloning yourself so you could play
out two lives at the same time? Maybe you wonder what it

would be like to be an Nigerian poet. To live in the country rather than the city. To be rich in New York. To be married to Ted Turner. To be younger. Older. Hipper. Richer. Poorer. Writing gives you the ability to enter into different worlds.

Some of our transformations occur because we reach a fork in the path and we take the road less traveled. The opposition between who you are and the opposite possibility can lead you to consider other alternatives for your characters.

THINK

Think about an incident in your life where you were at a crossroads. By choosing one path, you eliminated the other. Now imagine what experiences you would have had and who you would have become if you had chosen the other path. What would have happened if you had gone to that other college? Or gone abroad instead of staying in the U.S. for a summer? Or decided to date someone who turned out to be trouble, trouble, trouble? What if you had moved to one town instead of another?

How would your life be different? What skills or attitude or thoughts would you have now? How did the direction that you took influence you? What events have happened to you as a result of your choice? Imagine what would have happened if you had chosen the other route.

Think about a film in which a character had to make a choice. It might be *Working Girl* (to choose to impersonate her boss) or *Stake-Out* (to choose to try to date the woman he's observing) or *The Firm* (to choose to expose the corruption).

Choose a character from one of these films, or any
character who was confronted with a choice. Remember the choice or re-watch the film.

CREATE

Imagine that you've been hired to take the story in a
new direction by having your main character choose
differently. Write the scene. Then map out other
scenes that would change as a result of this choice.

You might want to watch the film *Sliding Doors* (by
Peter Howitt) to analyze parallel lives and cloning and different paths.

YOUR SCRIPT

What choices does your protagonist make in your
script? Who helps? Who hinders? Is your character
transformed? How and by whom?

Putting Opposition Into Dialogue

In great writing, the opposition between characters often
comes out in the relationship between the text and the
subtext in the dialogue. The text is what the character is
saying. The subtext is what the character really means.

In real life, we're often direct. We say exactly what we
mean. In drama, meaning is usually hidden in order to play
out more character layers and add opposition and tension.

Occasionally a character knows his or her subtext but
doesn't want to say it directly.

> THE TOUGH HOOD
> (in a saccharine tone)
> Don't worry about the money. It's not a problem
> to me.

If you only hear the text, you'll think, "What a swell guy to let me off the hook." But if you hear the subtext, you'll get the money fast, or it will be a problem to you.

Subtext asks, "What does the character really mean?" In many instances, subtext reveals character psychology, often what is unconscious and may be part of the shadow.

The most famous word in film history is the dying word of Charles Foster Kane in *Citizen Kane*: "Rosebud." The action of the movie tried to discover the literal meaning of the word "Rosebud." At the end of the film, we learned the subtextual meanings that the word carried for Kane—an untrammeled, more innocent time that Kane lost and could never recover.

In a *Cheers* episode, Frasier is supposed to be on television with Dr. Lilith Sternin. Frasier lets everyone in the bar know what he thinks about Lilith, and Diane proceeds to interpret the subtext of his remarks.

FRASIER
I have no intention of entering a debate with
those cold gray eyes and those clever smirking
lips. I'd rather clip my nails in a Cuisinart.

DIANE
Oh, my.

SAM
What's wrong?

DIANE
Oh, don't you see, Frasier's in love?

SAM
What?

> DIANE
> Oh come on, Sam. You're forgetting I was once ro-
> mantically involved with Frasier. I know when
> he's enamored with someone. Didn't you see his
> nostrils flare?[4]

She then goes on to prove that Frasier loves Lilith and Lilith loves Frasier.

When I was in graduate school, my friend Peggy was in love with John. She thought he loved her, although I had my doubts. One night at a dinner party, Peggy said, "I like this china," and John answered, "Yeah, it's sorta nice." Peggy interpreted that as meaning they had a lot in common and would surely get married. I saw it as a lack of interest.

Who was right? I was. Peggy didn't get the guy and didn't get the subtext.

Subtext is not just the underlying meaning of the dia-logue, but the relationship between the words, the body language, and the action. The person who says "nothing's wrong" while slamming the door is conveying the opposite of what is said. In *Gone With the Wind*, Charles Hamilton proposes to Scarlett, who has no interest in him. She wants Ashley. Scarlett catches a glimpse of Melanie and Ashley happy together, and immediately replies to Charles that she'll marry him. In this case, the audience realizes she's saying "yes" not because she wants Charles but because she can't have Ashley.

In good subtext, the melody doesn't match the lyrics. What is said and what is meant are not the same.

Discovering Subtext

Go to a restaurant or a mall or anyplace where you can observe people talking but are not close enough to them to hear what they're saying. Imagine what they're talking about by studying their body language—the energy between them, the gestures they use. Write the subtext that you think is being communicated, remembering that body language doesn't lie. (If you are around people who speak another language, you can try to interpret what they're saying by listening closely to the tone of their voices.)

Write the following scenes, conveying the subtext of the situation through the way the characters talk.

CREATE

A couple who is having marriage troubles goes into a mattress store to buy a bed. Although they seem to be talking about the mattress, they're actually communicating their anger to each other. Write the scene.

Remember, don't be too literal. Symbolize their feelings through the discussion of firmness, the size of the bed, the color of the bed, and the warranty. Be aware of possible subtextual meanings. What would the subtext be if one character pointedly says, "I never trust the warranties," and the other says, "It depends on whether you can trust the company to be loyal."

The relatives have stayed two days too long. You want to get rid of them, but you have to be nice because Uncle Jack is planning on leaving you his oil well. They think they'd be rude to leave too early. You want to convince them it's quite all right. Write the scene.

You see a gorgeous woman across the room, by the shrimp canapes. You wonder if she's married. If she's gay. If she's available. You start a conversation, discussing the buffet, but all the while your subtext is conveying your attraction and attempting to learn whether she's interested in you.

When writing the scenes, don't be "on the nose." Don't let the characters say the subtext. Hide the subtext.

Great characters are created through the use of conflict and subtext. These expressions of opposition will expand and deepen a character. They will also expand and deepen the writer. Great scripts do not spring from a vacuum. They come from writers who are willing to explore darkness, rough roads, confrontations in their journey toward transformation. This is where drama resides.

10.

Using Your Writing to Make
an Impact
. . . .

Why do you write? Do you have a desire or a goal that goes beyond money and acknowledgement and fame?

I was asked this question when I finished my last book, *When Women Call The Shots*. I laughed. "You want me to tell you my hidden agenda? It's to change the world as we know it. Why else would I write?"

Writing is not just personal expression. It's also communication. You don't write to put your work in an attic or to throw it away. You write to have it read and produced—to reach millions. You hope it has some effect beyond just being entertaining. You hope that an audience feels touched, inspired, changed.

My agenda for my six books has remained the same: To gain respect for all writers. I've grown a bit weary of the worn-out put-downs leveled against screenwriters—"it's not brain surgery." That cliché has gone far enough. I believe writing is as difficult and deserves the same respect as brain surgery or going to Mars or splitting the atom.

The screenwriter's lot in life is further complicated by the fact that many screenwriters fail to respect themselves. They want everything to be easy. They bypass the creative process. They copy and plagiarize and whine when a script takes longer than they think it should. I would like to see these perceptions about their art transformed. I'd like to see writers asking for the best from within themselves.

In Hollywood, the writer seems to receive the least respect of any of the principal contributors to a film. Everyone thinks s/he can write. And few respect experience. Producers have been known to say, "Don't send me a writer over thirty," as if writers are born, not made, and lose their ability with the onset of adulthood. Once producers do decide on a writer, they will whittle away at that writer's salary and adopt the attitude that one writer is interchangeable with another. While they may heap praise on the writer whose work is edgy and shocking and often derivative, producers rarely applaud the great writers who are authentic masters of their craft and art.

I'd like to see a change in the way that executives and producers and directors understand the writing process. I want them to understand the difficulty of the craft and appreciate the great achievements of great screenwriters.

Naturally, I don't expect that my books are going to change the world. But like many writers, I hope that my work has some effect. That it makes a difference.

Take a moment and think of the films that you believe are masterfully written. Think of the scripts that are your models. Think of the great screenwriters who can become your mentors. Here are a few of my favorite scripts by a few of my favorite contemporary writers.

Shakespeare in Love by Marc Norman and Tom Stoppard. "Brilliant!"

David Rayfiel is a master at rewriting who worked on *The Firm* and has many uncredited rewrites.

Steve Zaillian, writer of *Schindler's List* and *Searching for Bobby Fischer*, among others, is a genius!

I love Karen Croner's script of *One True Thing*. It's absolutely authentic and beautifully rendered.

Find your heroes and value them.

The Writer in a Social Context

Why do you write? Do you want to change the world? Touch and heal emotional pain? Raise consciousness? Shock audiences out of complacency? Transform a mind or a heart? Introduce us to new worlds and give us big visions?

Why do you continue to write? Because it matters.

We think of writing as expressing our individual identity. Of course it does that, but it expresses far more. What you put on paper is always a product of the world in which you live. You bring to your work your value system, your ethnicity, your economic class, your education, everything you've seen and done and are. You can't leave them behind.

WRITE

Write a short biography that describes your education, your travel experience, your family background, your academic and extracurricular interests, your ethnic background, your neighborhood.

REFLECT

Look at your scripts. What point of view comes across? Could someone who reads your work get a glimmer of who you are? Is your life in some way expressed through your work?

REFLECT

Have important parts of yourself gone unexplored in your writing? Have you explored your religion? Your political views? Your socials concerns? Note ways that you might explore these aspects of yourself in your future scripts.

YOUR SCRIPT

What social concerns come across in your script?
Are they clearly expressed? Do you tell them or
show them?

ACT

Go through the day with an attitude. Have opinions
about everything you see. Like this. Don't like that.
How dare they! That's terrible! That lacks integrity!
How corrupt! Feel deeply. Get passionate.

Your attitudes probably fall into three categories: You like some parts of your society. Critique others. Want to transform the rest.

Great writers express these three attitudes through their work.

Some writers accept and celebrate their social context:

Maybe you love the community in which you live. You celebrate small-town life—the close-knit family, the stability, the caring relationships between neighbors and friends (*The Wonder Years*).

You love the newspaper world. You don't love everyone in it, but you love the energy, the search for truth, the high stakes, the choices that must be made (*The Front Page, All the President's Men*).

You love your city—New York. What a place! You dislike Los Angeles—too superficial and glittery (most of Woody Allen's films).

Writing can break stereotypes, help us become more compassionate about people unlike ourselves, and expand our vision. What other cultures have you met through film that fascinate you? That have expanded your understanding of yourself and others? Some of the films that have touched me because they bring me into worlds unlike my own include:

Boyz N the Hood by John Singleton
The Joy Luck Club, screenplay by Amy Tan and Ron Bass
City of Joy by Mark Medoff
Philadelphia by Ron Nyswaner
Smoke Signals by Sherman Alexie
Eve's Bayou by Kasi Lemmons
Seven Years in Tibet by Becky Johnston
Driving Miss Daisy by Alfred Uhry

THINK

What films would be on your list?

WRITE

Write how you feel about the particular world and social context that you live in. Have you incorporated your feelings into any of your scripts? How might you?

OBSERVE

Go through a day and find all the parts of your culture that are humorous, dramatic, unique, interesting, and worth sharing.

Many scripts criticize and attack the culture, believing that it can be better.

Oliver Stone attacks the political structures and the lack of values in our culture. Sometimes he focuses on the manipulation of media (*Natural Born Killers*), the dishonesty and cover-ups (*JFK*), and the wrong decisions (*Platoon, Born on the Fourth of July*).

Some films attack the traditional and uncreative (*Dead Poets Society*). Some films attack religious practices and their hypocrisies (*Priests*, etc.). Woody Allen accepts and values his world of New York and enjoys throwing barbs at the illusions and superficiality of Hollywood.

REFLECT

Do you dislike parts of your culture? What problems do you see? Do any of your scripts express how you feel?

CREATE

As an exercise, create a character who feels the same way that you do. Write out the subtext for what that character would like to say about the culture. What's wrong with it? Who's to blame for what's wrong with it? What could be better?

WRITE

Now write the text of the scene, covering up the subtext using images, plot, character qualities to represent the theme. Don't hit us over the head with your attitude. Communicate your attitude without stating it directly.

To study masterful critiques of culture, look at *Dr. Strangelove, A Clockwork Orange, Jerry Maguire, Robocop, The Truman Show, Network, Wag the Dog, Bullworth, The Grapes of Wrath, Swept Away*.

Some writers not only critique their society, they want to change it. Some writers write about the possibilities of a better society. They see what's wrong and seek to tell its story, clarify its problems, and push their audiences into finding a solution. These writers write to expose the deception and corruption, to peer into falsehoods, to illuminate the darkness, hoping their truths will resonate with viewers who may feel the same way, but are unable to articulate their thoughts.

Television writers, even more than feature writers, deal with social issues. They work with ideas to help make society a safer, fairer, and better place to be. In some instances, what was hidden has been brought into the open, causing groups and individuals to push for new social structures, new laws. Attitudes are transformed and society changes.

Whether you actually saw the films *A Case of Rape* (written by Robert E. Thompson and aired in 1974) or *Something About Amelia* (written by William Hanley and aired in 1984) or The *Burning Bed* (written by Rose Leiman Goldemberg), you have, nevertheless, been living under the changes that occurred as a result of these films. No longer could our society take rape lightly, or could incest be kept in the shadows, or domestic abuse be ignored. The writers of these films changed society by telling the truth and exposing the problems in all their raw intensity, insisting, through the passions of their characters, that something be done. Something was done.

The desire to change society can be filled with pitfalls for the writer. Sometimes the desire to tell the truth can put you at loggerheads with your society and even with your potential market.

I once worked with a client who wanted to do an anti-abortion script and sell it to Hollywood. He was comfortable with his point of view, but it wasn't salable within the more liberal Hollywood community. That didn't mean that he shouldn't write the script—he simply needed to find another market.

You may remember the film *Fat Man and Little Boy*, about the dropping of the first atom bomb from the perspective of the men who dropped it. Few went to the film. I certainly had no interest in seeing a film about a horrific event that looked, from the previews, as if it was glamorizing the event or at least accepting it.

During the Gulf War, *Not Without My Daughter* was released, at a time when no one wanted to see more about the Middle East. It failed at the box office. Audiences had the opposite reaction to *The China Syndrome*. It was released the same week as the nuclear disaster at Three Mile Island. People crowded the theaters, wanting more explanations of what was happening. They felt as if they were in the middle of a great and important drama.

YOUR SCRIPT

Which do you do—celebrate, attack, transform?

Telling the Truth

The desire to tell the truth is a driving force for many writers. But truth-telling can be difficult. In rendering the truth, a writer can become black-and-white and polemic. The script can read like a message, not a story about human characters. The story can also become Pollyanna-ish and turn off an audience with its sweetness.

To work against this, the following exercises build on the materials you've worked with in the previous chapters—theme, the shadow, images, and creativity. You'll practice conveying your attitude toward society without hitting us over the head with your opinions. You'll convey your thoughts through dramatic action, not dialogue.

Choose a problem that you feel is out of control. Define it. You might decide: Sexuality is out of control among teenagers. If they're not careful, they'll all die of AIDS. Work on a definition of the problem until you have a clear statement.

Next, think about who will represent various sides of the argument. Who thinks that the free expression of sexuality needs to be stopped? You might have a fairly long list—parents, ministers, teachers, legislators, social service agencies, etc. Who is on the other side? Why? Some people might be adamantly against rigid rules, no matter what the consequences. Some educators might believe that sexuality is not the problem, it's non-consensual sex, and unsafe sex. Some drunk down the street, who couldn't care less about the issue, might just think the babes are cute. A parent might feel he can't set standards for his children because he's having an affair. Be flexible about this. Explore both sides of the issue.

Then, as you look at the characters who represent each side, ask yourself if their shadows are part of their viewpoints. The priest who is against all expressions of sexuality outside of marriage may be hiding his own sexual urges. Or maybe he's talking out of his own wisdom, learned from an affair that did damage to his soul. The mother might not want anyone to know she had a daughter out of wedlock and is unable to accept her shadow side. Or maybe she learned wisdom from her experience and has some creative solution to the problem based on her own experience. Don't go for the stereotype. Ask, "Whose shadow is speaking? Who has wisdom to offer?"

You will probably want to have a character who acts as your moral center, who brings wisdom and stability to your story. This might be a supporting character or the major character. This character can guide your story toward a possible answer.

You might want to show a transformation by creating a character who learns wisdom through a journey. Perhaps you have a character who starts out with out-of-control sexuality. Maybe s/he sleeps with someone who has AIDS. Show his/her journey to a value you believe is workable without being preachy. Be careful that these characters don't just represent one aspect of the problem, but contain complexities that can be expressed through their emotional lives. In drama, rarely is anything black and white. Be careful of creating cardboard characters who symbolize rigid ideas of right and wrong. That's fine for essays and for the pulpit, but it's not workable for dramatic writing.

YOUR SCRIPT

What issues do you explore? Do you use your characters to show both sides of these issues? Do this same exercise with your own script. Define the issue. Choose sides. Dimensionalize your characters.

Exploring Your Worlds

Each of us operates amid different social worlds. In our everyday life, we often move freely and comfortably from one to another. I'm a screenwriting teacher, a world traveler, a white, middle-class woman, a Quaker, a Christian, a horsewoman, a public speaker, a part of a neighborhood in Venice, California, an Angelino, a wife, a cat lover. Each of my worlds contains different kinds of people, and within these worlds are many subsets. As a Christian Quaker, my religious world is different than if I were a Baptist or Catholic. As an Angelino from Venice, my world is different than if I lived in Hollywood.

I have an attitude about each of my worlds. With some, I'm passionate. With others (such as living in Los Angeles), I'm ambivalent.

THINK

What are ten worlds that you're a part of? Perhaps they're the worlds of music, science, literature. Of a foreign culture. Of Protestantism. Of the literati.

Maybe you're a country gal or a New York-ish kind of guy.

WRITE

Write scenes that show three different stances toward these worlds: Celebrate them. Attack them. Transform them.

The desire to take one's own small idea and send it out to be manifested in the lives of millions is humankind's natural desire to communicate. Although writing is not just personal expression, it starts there.

Although some writers write and put their scripts into their garage, never to be seen by anyone else, most writers desire to get their work out there. Will society hear what you have to say? Will your work be accepted and valued? Will you be heard and understood? Will your work change anything? Will it matter?

Hopefully it will. But before you take that last step, consider another part of the process—spirituality—which is the subject of the next chapter.

11.

Connecting Your Spiritual Vision With Your Creative Work

Most writers find it difficult to articulate what happens to them during the act of creation. They say, "The idea just came to me." Or, "It feels as if creation is happening through me." Or, "I feel compelled to write." Or to borrow a line from *Shakespeare in Love*, "I don't know. It's a mystery."

In this chapter, I want to explore this mystery, looking at the relationship between our creative and spiritual selves. When creating, we need to be able to access all parts of ourselves. If your spirituality is an integral part of your life, then to leave it behind when writing weakens your voice and robs you of an opportunity to enrich your creative self and your spiritual self through your work.

I am aware, in writing a chapter on creativity and spirituality, that some readers will be turned off by a discussion that includes concepts of God, religion, theology, and spirituality. If you're one of those readers, you may want to skip this chapter.

However, I have been studying this relationship for more than thirty years, first when working on an M.A. in drama, then later as a seminary student where I received an M.A. and Th.D in Drama and Theology, and always as a creator, recognizing that my creative self is constantly being nurtured by my spiritual self.

The Act of Creation

Most major religions have a creation story. When we create, our process as creators is similar to the process of the Creator(s).

In some creation stories, creation does not come from nothingness, but gives form to something that was once formless. In the Judeo-Christian religions, the Word brings forth the world, beginning with Light (inspiration and illumination) and giving shape and substance to matter. The Word spoken, the word on the page, begins the process.

Like the Creator, the artist also builds and shapes and brings new worlds into being. In some ways, the two closest art forms to this work of the Spirit are sculpture and writing.

The sculptor takes clay and gives it form, sometimes even breathing life into it, as Geppetto did with Pinocchio and Pygmalion did with his Galatea and Dr. Frankenstein did with his monster and God did with Adam.

Fiction writing creates human forms by incarnating the word into character. Screenwriting and playwriting go a step further. Actors become the character, bringing this new human being to life.

In the Jewish mystical tradition described in the Kabbalah, there is another part to the process. In one interpretation, The Divine Energies pull back or contract to make room for the world and to allow human beings free will. God steps back, just as the writer also has to pull back and let his or her characters speak and act and find their way. Just as God is invisible, the writer also has to be invisible. It is a letting go—while still remaining in relationship with the creation. Free will, and choosing to relinquish control, are part of the process.

Just as many creation accounts say that we are made in the image of the Creator, so too are your characters created in your image. They incarnate your values and ideas and insights and experiences. Your work as a writer is to breathe life into your characters and to make them count for something. You are making something out of that which is without form—a vague theme, the slight stirring of some new idea, the beginning images, the shady outline of a character. You are showing us what you think is important about the human being, about the human condition, about a character's relation to his or her culture. And, hopefully, you do it with a love of humanity, which is at the heart of most world religions and spiritual practices.

REFLECT

Do you have a favorite creation story (or stories)? How does this creation story relate to your own experience as a creator?

Creation as a Sacred Act

Intrinsically, the act of creation is a sacred act. Some writers talk about being "called" to do their work. Others about getting a spiritual high from writing or about feeling that they are adding important value to the world or about being guided by some Higher Self or Spiritual Muse. I believe that creativity comes from this Spirit. We are able to stay with the creative struggle because we feel empowered or guided by something bigger, higher, greater, better within ourselves. This sacred relationship is an experience, not just a belief system. Although the vocabulary changes from person to person, it's not unusual for writers to sense that there is Something or Someone behind their work.

For many, this relationship is personal. We experience a guiding presence that cares for and nurtures our work.

Others see this spiritual relationship as a river or movement or flow. Many writers desire a deeper connection with this Source in order to further build up and shape and bring meaning to their work.

In Relationship With the Source

For some writers, the experience of the creative act feels like the Muse moving them into a type of superhuman concentrated ecstatic state. They recognize that part of the creative process is visionary.

Most writers who experience the Spirit behind their work recognize that life is made up of profound, transcendent experiences that touch them and change them. It is these transformative experiences that they wish to explore and express, hoping to leave the world a better place because of their creations. This might mean bringing hope to audiences or giving a new perspective on life, or revealing the possibilities of life. Their work serves truth and cares for the humanity they're shaping. They feel that they've touched some layer of life that can be as important to our world as the monk or the healer or those social activists who work in the service of some Higher Power. Many sense that, somehow, their small efforts are important. They are able to continue because they feel connected to Someone who guides and cares.

Tapping into this underlying spiritual source of creativity is visualized in different ways. If, for instance, you're a fundamentalist Christian, you may see this relationship as trying to find out God's will for your next script. If you're a Presbyterian, you may even feel predestined to be a screenwriter.

In a contemporary theology called Process Theology, which I find particularly appealing, our individual creative spirit and the larger Creative Spirit work together to build up and develop creation. This is an unfolding process of dialogue between our work and the life-giving work of the Spirit. We are constantly building on the work of history and the new information and insights that we observe every day, finding new combinations and working with the Spirit to bring meaning to our ideas. The Creative Spirit uses our choices and responds to our choices. What was created last week or last year is used to form new creations. Process theology believes that, just as we change as a result of tuning into this Source, this Source can also change as a result of our creative work. We work together to make something new.

Either way you look at it, the Spirit cherishes our unique gifts, and we cherish the Spirit who created these gifts, encourages us, and breathes life-giving ideas into us.

REFLECT

Do you experience a Presence that is behind your work? Do you experience a dialogue between you and the Spirit as you write? If so, write about it, articulating how this relationship nurtures your creative work.

Creation as a Gift

In the way I view the world and my work, creation is a gift and a blessing. It comes from the Life-Giver, so our response as creators is to create something that is life-giving. We hope to leave the world a better place because our work enlivens or heals or affirms those who see it. A test of this meaning might be: Did we experience the transcendent in a creative work? Was there something good and meaningful that expanded and enriched our lives? Was it worth sitting in the theater for two hours, or was it a waste of time and a robbing of our Spirit?

Although how we experience a film can vary, some of the diverse films where I experienced the transcendent include *Schindler's List, The Associate, Pulp Fiction, Sense and Sensibility, Shine, The Apostle, Witness, Tender Mercies, Driving Miss Daisy*. In some of these films, my compassion was awakened. In others, hope. In some, such as *Pulp Fiction* or *Schindler's List*, a character was transformed unexpectedly, even miraculously. Some, such as *Tender Mercies, Witness, The Associate*, showed me the strength and care of community. Some, such as *The Apostle* and *Shine*, showed me the struggle for redemption, and affirmed my own struggle.

By nurturing our spiritual selves, we are more able to create transcendent experiences in films. This nurturing can then make our work more meaningful, deeper, more joyful, richer.

REFLECT

Have you ever meditated about the relationship between your creative work and the work of the Creative Spirit? Have you ever prayed for the Creative Spirit to enrich and enliven your creative work? Have you asked for guidance: "What would You have me do? What would You have me write about?"

Giving Shape/Building Up

Creation is a natural act. We don't go against our natures or against God's nature by creating. Whereas some theologians and psychologists say that inertia and procrastination and fear are natural to the human state, I take the opposite view. I, and many others, believe that creating and innovating and adding something new to our world is one of the most natural acts that we can do. We do it as children, when our natural desires are to reach out, to discover, to experiment, to try out, to see the world from a fresh perspective. We do it when we form new relationships and reach out and allow ourselves to be transformed by others, whether they be teachers, friends, or lovers. The blocks and limitations from fear, resistance, and rigidity hold us back from becoming whole and expressive people.

In the Hebrew-Christian story, creation is Good. In the Isis religion, which originated in ancient Egypt, Isis pairs destruction and creation together, by breathing life into the fourteen broken body-parts of her consort, Osiris. She didn't allow total destruction to stop her, just as some writers manage to breathe new life into the broken pieces of their work.

In the Hindu Trinity of Brahma (Creator), Vishnu (Preserver), and Shiva (Destroyer), darkness and destruction are not seen as separate from God, but another aspect of the God-head. The three forces must maintain a balance. Destruction must clear the way for creation. As a writer, you prune and destroy some of what doesn't work to create and preserve what does.

Some writers relate to the idea that to create, you sometimes need to destroy. To build up, you sometimes need to tear down. The positive and the negative are not divided, but part of the same process. For some writers, the intention is not to build up to something good and transformational and positive, but to do good by showing the negative, the destructive, the dysfunctional, the shadowy underside that lies beneath and is an integral part of life. Some believe that only by exposing the negative can anything positive, either within their characters or within an audience, be achieved.

Both of these systems recognize an underlying truth about life—either about struggle and pain or about possibilities and redemption.

Depending on the religious system that guides you, you will choose what you create and reveal by what you see as your creative mission—to build up the good, reveal the negative, or show the transforming possibilities no matter how great the evil.

You can see that our discussion in Chapter Ten about your relation to your culture is also part of your relation to the spirituality that guides you.

REFLECT

What do you see as your creative mission? Do you want to explore the shadow or explore the light? How do you do it by recognizing the reality of both?

The Spiritual Struggle of Creation

No one said it would be easy. As human beings, we desire to do things our own way. We don't tap into our Inner Power. We misinterpret and go off in wrong directions. We have our own sense of timing and get angry when our process doesn't evolve according to our timetable.

And, of course, our work is often not appreciated by others—such as our society, or the executives, producers, and directors who are supposed to buy our work or the audiences who don't come en masse to our brilliant creations that are meant to change the world.

I have heard some writers say that this resistance to their work is the work of Satan or of evil in the world. This concept is not part of my theology, but I admit that many obstacles (many of them internal, some external) keep our creations from having an easy time of it. Many oppositional forces try to keep our work from coming to fruition and from making its way in the world. Psychoanalyst Eric Neumann, in *Creativity and the Unconscious*, calls these forces rigidity and chaos. He sees them as evil, as part of the major forces that oppose good. Although I don't define them as evil, since that leaves out any possibility of reconciling or integrating opposition, I do agree with him that rigidity and chaos are the major oppositional forces to any creative writer.[1]

It seems to be woven into the fabric of our human lives that we want our lives to include the familiar, the stable, the dependable, the trustworthy. This is normal. But when these normal desires become solidified into convention and a conservatism that resists change, they become the enemy of the creative process. They are reactive rather than pro-active. They create the critical voice that diminishes and degrades the work of the artist and resists the basic work of the creator—to make it new.

Psychologist Mihaly Csikszentmihalyi says, "Each of us is born with two contradictory sets of instructions: a conservative tendency, made up of instincts for self-preservation, self-aggrandizement, and saving energy and an expansive tendency made up of an instinct for exploring, for enjoying novelty and risk—the curiosity that leads to creativity belongs to this act. We need both of these programs. But whereas the first tendency requires little encouragement or support from outside to motivate behavior, the second can wilt if it is not cultivated. If too few opportunities for curiosity are available, if too many obstacles are placed in the way of risk and exploration, the motivation to engage in creative behavior is easily extinguished."[2]

This resistance can come from inside ourselves, when we feel diminished by judgment—our own or others—when we lack the discipline to affirm our own unique voice, when we are afraid to be daring and bold. It can lead to entropy, inertia, procrastination, and a dead halt. This resistance can also come from others who have the power to buy our work and think it's too different, too unique, when what they're really looking for is a *Driving Miss*

Daisy meets *Independence Day.* The business side of show business can easily see the creative act in terms of the mass market, in terms of numbers and dollars and overseas sales. This resistance can come from audiences who want to see the same rehashed film because, unfortunately, even the audiences' desire for innovation has been stifled.

Reviewers can appeal to our conventionalism and toss anything new aside by marginalizing it, trivializing it, deciding it's not important enough.

I'm not at all sure that we can overcome this resistance unless we have some sense of a spiritual force that's on our side, that encourages our efforts, that believes in us, that inspires us and moves us. When we believe that our work is important and meaningful, and sense an inner affirmation to our belief, we're able to continue.

When fame comes to us, we're able to resist the seduction of materialism and the trap of an inflated ego if we look at our success from a spiritual perspective. Our perspectives remain in balance when we recognize that our work is not solely our creation, but a gift we give because of the gift we've received.

Whereas rigidity is a negative life force, transformation is a positive life force. All the natural processes of life are about growth—from birth to death. The development into physical and mental and spiritual maturity, illness giving way to health, the transformation of attitudes and relationships and points of view, from conversions and crises to the accumulation of knowledge and the solving of problems—all is transformation.

The work of the Creator is building, changing. When we create, our work is part of this process—to go with the flow of life, to resist the forces that try to bring us to a stop.

Just as rigidity can be an opposing force, so can chaos. We know of threats that can pull our world into disorganization, into violence, into destruction, or as poet Willam Butler Yeats said, "The center cannot hold."[3] Chaos is the beginning of all creative work, but it's not meant to be the end.

Our work is to bring order to chaos, without negating it. In the Chinese symbol of the Tao (the black-white, yin-yang symbol), light and dark, male and female, and chaos and order are held in a tension and a balance. It is the perfection of the duality. We don't smooth over chaos or reject it, but we bring patterns and meaning to it to see and understand it more clearly.

If you visualize the Tao symbol, you may remember that it has a black dot on the white background, and a white dot on the black background. The stable quiet of the dots in the center of the swirling forms exemplify the most creative position of the writer—a quiet center or eye in the hurricane, observing and using the energy of chaos to create new forms.

When we are constantly brought back into chaos, we make no headway. The story remains a muddle. What we do makes no sense. We remain in confusion.[4] But when we understand that the creative process is always in flux and learn to live with the tension between chaos and order, we are better able to illuminate reality.

As creators we stand on the boundary between these two opposing forces—rigidity and chaos. How to reconcile these two? Sometimes we're part of the problem. We want the easy solution, the quick result, and are unrealistic about the life we have chosen.

Some of this difficulty is with us. Some writers expect their first script to sell "by God's Grace," not by their own work and preparation and knowledge and imagination. Some write scripts that are beyond their abilities to pull off. Some believe that it's God's job to make everything go our way. But, this is not a perfect world and there is nothing that says it must be easy. We will struggle and there will be opposition and our creation will not reach fruition solely through our own work. The universe does not stand or fall by whether we write our ten pages this morning, but our work can add or subtract in some small or large way to the overall scheme of things.

EXERCISES

Before your write, take some time to pray or meditate about the work you are about to do. This prayer might be sitting and centering into the Creative Source, or it might be a very specific prayer for the character you're about to bring to life, the story you're trying to tell, the images and themes you're trying to express. One of my favorite Quaker theologians, Douglas Steere, recommends that we pray about everything, and if it's an egocentric prayer, in the process, God will change our prayer.[5]

If you're stuck in your writing, you might do an exercise that I've done whenever I'm overwhelmed by the task at hand and my writing comes to a dead halt. I give myself up to three days to get over being scared. Then, the night before the third day, I have a discussion with God, simply stating that I know that I have to get back to writing the next day, and really don't feel capable of doing it, but I'm asking for help. Without fail, the next morning, I feel fresh and excited about the writing and ready to write.

I also try to put the work into perspective. Like the AA member who simply prays to get through each day with God's help, I pray to get through the task for the day. I often ask, "How does one write a book?" The answer is one word at a time. I don't have to deal with the whole book, only with one day's worth.

Dealing With Rejection and Fear

Your spiritual life becomes particularly important when your work is done and ready to go out and you feel desperate and afraid. The creative life involves more than its share of disappointments, struggles, sheer terror, confusion, frustration—and that's only the writing. When you finish and turn it out into the world, what follows is usually rejection, disappointments, some abuse, injustices, unfairness, a few insults, more struggle. You're misunderstood, not listened to, not cared about, sometimes trampled underfoot. Lots of barriers exist between you and success. Without some perspective that can come from seeing it all from a spiritual point of view and recognizing that this is the state of affairs on Earth, it's much too easy to become cynical and embittered or to give up.

Through our sense of connection with the Sacred, we recognize that creation is not complete. Every word we write, every thought we have, every image we create, every character we birth—all are part of the power the Creator has given us to continue to build up and shape creation.

It is, for me, a powerful thought, that this, too, can be part of a larger design. And when my work is put into the world, I can't know the good that it might do. More than once I've been surprised how one of my books has touched someone, even though I've wondered if it's making its way. More than once, a film that might have seemed small and insignificant seems to make a difference with the people who see it. Knowing that success is not just measured in money or numbers also takes us into a different reality of a higher and deeper value.

I believe that the Creative Spirit and the Holy Spirit are integrally connected to each other, that the source of our creativity is the Spirit that is within us and also transcends us. When I received my Th.D. in Drama and Theology, my graduation speaker was Nelle Morton, whose speech was

titled "Holy Spirit, Woman Spirit, Child Spirit, Creative Spirit."
Using Janusian thinking, you may want to morph these four
images together. Might this not be how some creators, all
through history, have experienced the Muse?

I believe that the creative work that builds up, that expresses both the shadow and the transformation, flows
from God. Just as this Spirit is implicit in any action that is
kind, compassionate, just, fair, and loving, so also is this Spirit
implicit in the creative acts that tell the truth, express the
transcendent, give hope, and deeply care about humanity.
The writer, when striving for the highest and deepest level,
allows the Spirit to manifest itself within his or her work.

12.

How to Get Quality Feedback to Improve What You've Written

Many writers believe the creative process is finished when they finish the script. They forget the essential last stage of the process—verification.

Up to this time, you've been expressing yourself, finding your personal voice, getting your ideas onto the page. But writing is more than personal expression. It's also communication. Your audience should receive your story's message clearly and sense the same passion that you felt when writing it.

As you've read this book, hopefully, you've been able to remove the 13th floor from your process—the floor where the KGB, the judgmental parent, the critical peers and picky co-workers live. Now it's time to evaluate your work.

As you've been working, the inner evaluator has undoubtedly popped up now and then. Sometimes it comes with a feeling of exhilaration: That felt good today. Seems better than what I saw on TV last week. Wow! This is the best I've done! At other times it fills you with fear and trepidation and confusion: Where do I go from here? Will I ever get this right? It's not working. Should I give up?

You stare out the window for hours. Get that old sinking feeling that your script is dreadful. You get anxiety attacks. You wonder if you're capable of pulling this off.

This inner evaluator gives you hints and the prickly sensation that leads you to your first set of changes. Maybe it takes you through several rewrites, reworking and honing and changing and experimenting.

REFLECT

Look at your story or script or a scene that you've written. Where does it work well? Does your intuition tell you that some part of it doesn't work? Try to articulate your feelings.

What was your intention? By reiterating your intention, do you get some ideas of what to rewrite?

Do you have concerns about your script? Have you lost your passion for it? Are you wondering if it's any good at all?

If so, open the letter that you wrote in Chapter One. Let the letter reawaken your passion, your vision, your excitement about your work. Let the letter guide you during this last stage of the process, as you match up your script with your original vision of it.

Be Open to Outside Feedback

Some writers reject any criticism. They're in love with their every word, believe it's perfect, and no one will tell them any differently. Those writers rarely sell their work. If they sell it, they fight with the producer and director and the executives who dare to change a line. They become known as "difficult." When the film is released, audiences sense that something is not quite working. They tell their friends, "Don't go, it's not that good!"

I've been in more than one difficult meeting when the writer refused to change anything. They were uphill battles, in spite of a consensus by all involved that the scripts didn't work. In one instance, an executive told me, "He's a good writer, but he's not worth the aggravation. We're not going to work with him again." Another time, the executives who planned on buying the script decided not to. In another, an animation film actually began the production process and was canceled. In another, the company had a production date, but the film was pulled about two months before filming began.

In each of these instances, the writer's refusal to work collaboratively ruined his or her career in spite of the writer's talent and fascinating story. The writer didn't understand that the last step of the process is verification by outside readers, executives, and eventually audiences.

Great writers rewrite, again and again. I asked my writing friend Treva Silverman how many times she rewrites. "An infinite number. Yesterday, I rewrote one scene about twenty times."

Why? "I was feeling the character wouldn't use those exact words. I needed to know what he was thinking and feeling each moment: When he thought of a particular word in the sentence. Where he changed his mind. What he was hiding."

The more experienced you are, the more your inner evaluator might be able to take you through a number of rewrites. But even great writers go outside for input.

REFLECT

How do you feel about input from others? Does the thought make you feel defensive? Are you afraid? Do you wonder if they'll be truthful?

If you're defensive, you cut off any dialogue and any possibility of receiving help. Remember, they're not attacking you personally, but they might be attacking your script. Take a deep breath and entertain the possibilities they're suggesting.

But where do you go? Whom can you trust?

Begin With Readers

Most writers begin by asking friends and colleagues to read their work. You might choose friends, screenwriting colleagues, your writers' group or class.

Be careful whom you ask. Be careful of feedback that makes you despair rather than gives you hope. Be careful of readers who are going to tear you down and use their ego to let you know how inferior, insufficient, and incapable you are. You don't need that. No matter how bad your first draft is, it is never worthy of disdain. You need constructive, specific, caring feedback. Choose wisely.

> *REFLECT*
>
> Make a list of five or ten readers whom you think would be helpful. What are their talents as evaluators? Do they know enough about screenwriting to be helpful, or will you need to clarify what EXT. DAY means?

A first evaluation may be confusing. Perhaps you'll receive feedback like that which appears in the following scene from Treva Silverman's adaptation of renowned playwright Moss Hart's memoir, *Act One*.

EXT. BEACH—DAY

Early Autumn. Moss sits writing, a pile of ten composition books by his side.

He writes:

"The curtain falls."

He pauses, puts at the bottom:

"September 3, 1925."

He picks up his notebooks, packs everything up, walks over to the edge of the water.

                    MOSS
                   (softly)
        Whatever's out there...or not...thank you for giv-
        ing me this...you know...this gift...this talent...to
        express myself, to hopefully influence others.
        Thank you.

He leans down, picks up a seashell, joyously throws it into the ocean. As it spins in the air, we hear:

                EDDIE's VOICE (V.O.)
        It's shit.

                                              CUT TO:

INT. TEXAS STEAK HOUSE—NIGHT

                    MOSS
        Oh.

                    BOBBY
        Jesus, it's a nice first play. You don't say to some-
        body his first play is shit.

                    EDDIE
        (to Moss) Excuse me. It's a gem. A rare diamond.
        That reads surprisingly like shit.

MOSS

Come on. I can take it. If it's shit, it's shit. Let's just
all declare it's shit.

Dead silence.

MOSS

(groans) Oh, God.

BOBBY

Hey, what do I know? I'm an actor. Actors just
count their lines. I really shouldn't comment.

STAN

(nervously) And I'm...just halfway through.

EDDIE

Right. Halfway through. Excuse me, but haven't
you been halfway through for the past two days?
(to Moss) Look, are you interested in a little honesty around here?

MOSS

Of course! How can you even ask?

EDDIE

All right. The dialogue. People don't talk that way.
Unless it's a play about Mars, where it may be
breathtakingly accurate.

MOSS

(nods) Uh huh. Uh huh. Good.

EDDIE

The plot—is utterly predictable. It's like sing-
along-with-the-plot, you know hours in advance
what's going to happen. Why didn't you just write

a description of brushing your teeth, there
would've been more surprises. Up, down, up,
down...

MOSS
(nods) Uh huh. Uh huh. Good.

EDDIE
The characters... blur, blur, blur. I couldn't tell one
from the other. They all sounded the same, like
people who had graduated first in their class at
cliché school. Now if you could only think of
some way of marketing it as a sleeping pill—

MOSS
(pause)
How do you like the typing?

After this difficult beginning, Moss Hart went on to write
many other plays, including "The Man Who Came to Dinner," "Lady In The Dark," and "You Can't Take It With You,"
which won the Pulitzer Prize in 1936. He also wrote many
screenplays, including *Gentlemen's Agreement* and *A Star
Is Born.*

REFLECT

What kind of feedback have you received about your
writing? If you had to write a scene about an evaluation you've received, how would your scene differ
from Treva's?

How do you judge feedback, when some seem to love
your script, some seem lukewarm, some have that dreaded
subtext in their voice that implies, "I don't like it but I can't
tell you that, so I'll just say 'good start.'" You get comments
like "Yeah, there were some good things there." Or "Well,
you finished!" or "It looks professional." Others might say,

"I love the main character" or "Why did he have to go to Tibet?"You might decide to ignore the bad and choose the good—which won't resolve the overall problem with your script. Or you might decide to rewrite according to the comments, but find they're so vague and unfocused that you're not sure how to proceed.

Many readers are unable to sort through the raw first draft, when the writing is sloppy and the dialogue still wooden.They think you're in the final rewrite and pick at every badly written description. Knowing this, some writers wait too long for feedback, traveling down some unworkable road and wasting months in the process. Having feedback after a first draft can be helpful. A reader might find an underdeveloped theme that could be further explored. Or think of a story twist that might make your script more exciting.

With friends and colleagues, the kind of evaluation you receive will cover a wide spectrum. General feedback—"I liked it/didn't like it"—is only marginally useful. If they don't like it, you'll be immobilized for weeks. If they do like it, you'll feel happy and perky but wonder whether they liked everything or just generally liked the concept.

Some readers will give you page-by-page notes when it's still in a rough draft. That's great feedback after a few rewrites, but you don't need it now.

Others will tell you specifics about their area of expertise—either about characters or structure or dialogue.This can be useful, but it will only cover a small part of the script. You might find out that your lead character is good, but you still won't know anything about the structure or story.

When asking non-professional readers for feedback, ask them to have a dialogue with your material. Suggest they make notes in the margin, letting you know that they like this scene, like this character, this scene seems unnecessary, this is confusing, this is exciting, this doesn't seem to flow. You can ask them to cross out what seems over-written or unnecessary or irrelevant. Tell them you want to know where it soars.

Writing out a checklist of questions can be a good way to get feedback from non-professional readers.

Here are some questions you might ask readers, depending on which draft of the script they're reading:

For rough drafts, in the early stages of development:

> Is the basic concept interesting? Fresh? Something you'd want to see in a movie? What parts of the story did you find compelling? Original? Dramatic? Intriguing? Did any parts of the story confuse you? Who were your favorite characters? Which ones felt most alive to you? Which ones seemed stereotypical? Was the main character interesting and believable? What do you think the script was about? What theme did you feel I was communicating? What did you find the most memorable about the script? If it's a comedy, did you find it funny? If it's supposed to be suspenseful, was it?

When the script has gone through several drafts, and you think you've nailed the story, you might ask:

> Does it work? Is it clear? Focused? Well-structured?
> Did the story hold you?
> Where did you feel your attention wane?
> Did the story seem cinematic? Could you visualize it as you read it?
> Did you find the main character sympathetic?
> Did you understand his/her motivations?
> Was the concept intriguing?
> Did it make you think of other related ideas?
> Can you think of other ideas I should consider?

Perhaps another twist to the story? Something
else to add to a character? Can you think of any
touches that would make it more commercial?

Just as you're ready to get your script to market, you
might want a few more sophisticated readers to look at it,
perhaps screenwriters who have sold some of their work.
Questions for these readers might include:

Does the overall narrative read well? Did the writing
bog down anywhere?
Did the dialogue seem realistic? Were there any
places where it seemed wooden? Too conventional?
Lacked subtext?
Are there any places that are over-written or
repetitive?

YOUR SCRIPT

What are some questions you'd like to ask your
readers about your script?

If you can find good positive readers who can brainstorm ideas with you early in the verification stage, great.
If you're getting nothing but criticism, just stop. Find someone else, or follow your heart for another draft.

Sometimes, you're fortunate enough to have gotten the
script working well by the time you go for outside feedback. If five or ten readers all tell you that it's wonderful,
and you feel it's wonderful, then go ahead and get it out
there. But this is rare. The normal course of events is to get
feedback that's either negative and useless, partly confusing, or wonderful, which gets you back on track.

My Own Evaluation Process

You've almost finished reading this book. You've had an opportunity to enter into your creative process through it. You are also seeing the result of my creative process, including the impact of feedback and evaluation from a number of readers. I thought you might find it helpful to see how this process worked.

The first draft of this book flowed well. I was often awakened in the middle of the night or early in the morning with ideas rushing at me. Several months after I signed the contract, I was surprised how much I had written just working on weekends, during part of the summer, and on some of my trips. During this time, I also continued to research, reading or skimming about fifty books on the creative process, which reinforced the work I began in 1972 when I started studying creativity.

The difficulty in my creative process came at the verification stage. The main question my readers asked: "Who is your audience?" Some of the book seemed to address the beginning writer, some addressed the more experienced writer. Some of my readers were very experienced writers who felt the book held nothing for them. I continued to show them chapters, trying to find if anything in this book could be helpful to them. Finally, after several rewrites, they began to respond to the chapters on character, metaphor, shadow, theme, and spirituality. They then suggested that I add quotes about the creative process from well-known writers, believing that new writers would want to know how the great ones did it, and more experienced writers would want to know what their peers do.

All my readers had a big problem with my original first chapter, which was about getting started. They found it far too basic. Finally I cut it out and threaded necessary information into my chapters on creativity.

Much of the feedback was confusing. Although readers would tell me something was wrong, they weren't able to tell me what it was. I became immobilized, sometimes even angry because of their negativity. I finally analyzed each reader's abilities to figure out what each could give me. Some were very good at ideas for formatting the exercises. Another at line-by-line editing. Several gave me more general comments, but good emotional support. Some gave me ideas about processes they used but I hadn't included. Other readers enthusiastically did the exercises and would let me know what worked and what didn't.

When I became very confused with the feedback, I went to my literary consultant, Dr. Lenny Felder. Lenny heard my despair, understood my vision, and was able to pinpoint what he felt was going wrong with the readers and with the writing. He felt that I wasn't writing enough from my viewpoint as a script consultant. He helped me tune into the problems that I've observed with my writing clients and clarify why each chapter was important to overcome those problems. He encouraged me to think of specific clients who had struggled with specific issues. He told me to rework the first pages of each chapter and clarify the importance of the chapter and consequences for writers if they don't master visual thinking or learn to work with the shadow or learn structure or oppositional thinking. Lenny is terrific with titles (which I'm not) and not only gave me the title for the book, but helped me develop more provocative titles for each chapter.

The last problem I had to deal with was the chapter on spirituality. I sent the chapter to people from thirteen different spiritual backgrounds to make sure it was not a turn-off for any of them. For the last four weeks of rewriting, I worked with Lenny and four readers who were willing to turn around chapters fairly quickly and keep giving me feedback.

No matter what feedback you receive, take it seriously. If several people say something is wrong, chances are it is. This initial feedback can let you know that your work is not ready to go into the marketplace. That doesn't mean that the reader knows how to fix it. Many people in this industry, including high-level executives, admit to knowing what's wrong but don't have a clue what to do about it. Even if your readers know how to fix part of your script, that doesn't mean they're skilled at integrating all the aspects of the script. When you reach a stopping point with your readers, consider hiring a professional script consultant.

Professional Feedback

I began my script-consulting business in 1981 because I saw the need for more specific feedback. I had developed my consulting method as part of my doctoral dissertation project and knew it helped pinpoint problems. Since the late 1980s, fifty to seventy other individuals have also taken up this career. Some of them are good, some are not.

When hiring a script consultant, be careful whom you choose. Don't collude with a critical parent by allowing him or her to exercise his or her ego and his or her self-righteousness on your work. There are those who love to criticize work, to tear it down, to tell you everything that's wrong with it. You don't need that and it won't help your creativity.

Your consultant shouldn't be part of the 13th floor of the KGB, but part of the top floor. This is the floor where the Masters of the Craft reside—the mentors and wise and insightful guides. Their job is to help you evaluate the material and help you follow your vision.

Many screenwriters who call me for consulting begin their conversations, "I think it's good, but there's something not working and I don't know what it is." Experienced writers often call me to help evaluate such subtleties as

tone or humor, saying, "My script is too dark and I want to
lighten it. I have some ideas, but I want a professional objective eye."

The evaluation you're looking for works on many levels. You first want to know whether you've achieved your
intention. If you defined your goal as, "I want to create a
broad romantic comedy that also has profound insights into
the nature of romance," then you want your consultants to
tell you that they laughed and also learned something new.
If they didn't, don't decide "that's just them." You probably
haven't achieved your goal.

A good consultant should be specific. S/he should tell
you clearly what works and what doesn't work, whether
your creation has gotten off track, reached a dead-end. A
good consultant should help you understand how to integrate all the elements of your script. S/he can clarify
whether you got your soul and passion into your work. S/he
can give you suggestions about how to re-think your intention, create a different ending or beginning, pull out a
theme, or expand on an image. Sometimes this means minor
rewriting and some clarification. Sometimes it means dras-
tic re-thinking of the story, doing much more research, or
cutting or changing characters.

Some script consultants are also writing coaches. They
can guide you through a rewriting process as writing mentors. If you're a first-time writer, that can be a very valuable process.

Don't make your consultant into a god or a guru. Naturally, it's flattering for us, but we're not here to be flattered,
but to turn you back to your own creativity and awaken
what's great within you. Turn to a consultant for honest,
supportive feedback, for an objective eye, for a knowledge
of the craft and for a cherishing of your creative process
and growth as a writer. Consultants can help you on this
important last step of verification.

REFLECT

What questions would you ask to evaluate a pro-
spective script consultant? Here are some possibilities: What is his/her background? Most script
consultants are also writers and teachers. Find out
what they've written, where they've taught, and
what they consider to be their specialty. Listen to
hear if the consultant you're considering runs everyone else down. If so, s/he might just as easily run you
down. You might ask for references and call other
clients. Find out what others say about the
strength and weaknesses of the consultant.

Verification Through Sale

The next stage of evaluation will come from the producers and directors and actors and executives and agents who
read your script and evaluate their own passion for your
work.

You always hope that these outside evaluators will tell
you, "I love it—let's make a deal." That's the dream. But
you're more apt to hear, "It's not the kind of material we're
looking for this year." A producer will never tell you the
writing is awful, the story dull, the characters one-dimensional, and you don't know how to format. In Hollywood,
most people reject you with kindness because, if you write
a great next script, they don't want you to go elsewhere to
make your hit. They want to keep the door open, just in
case. The evaluative code of Hollywood would consider it
rude to tell the truth about an unworkable script.

REFLECT

Do you know any professionals in the business who
might be interested in your script? List people you
know, or who you know who knows someone.

As a writer, you need to sort through Hollywood's own evaluative code. You've been evaluating whether it's art, whether it works, whether you got your vision on the page. They're evaluating whether it's commercial.

What Is Commercial?

No one really knows. The studio believes a great script makes a lot of money, and it tries to choose scripts they think will be box-office hits. They're often wrong in their predictions. The director might consider a great script the one that will entice Sharon Stone or Robert De Niro or Brad Pitt to play the lead. The producer might consider the great script the one that can bring in the investors. The critics may look for originality and innovation, the audience for excitement and unforgettable characters. Some of the finest scripts may not make money. Occasionally scripts recognized as pure drek by almost everyone except the financier make a bundle.

This does not mean that no one knows anything. It does mean that there is no way you can write to Hollywood's idea of commerciality. They don't know what it is. How can you figure it out? You can, however, learn to evaluate whether the buyer is most apt to be a studio or a small independent production company.

Evaluate your script by asking:

Is it an intriguing story with unexpected twists and turns and surprises and unpredictabilities? (If so, it could sell through the studios or the independent market.)

Is it so dark that its audience may be limited? (If so, if it's a well-written script and can be made on a low budget, you may be able to sell it through the independent market.)

Is it expensive? (If it's expensive, It has to be a studio picture.)

Is it castable? (Studios will want the top stars, but some independent scripts are so well done that they can attract great stars looking for a more original roles.)

Is it original enough to attract an A-list director and top box-office stars? (If so, your market is the studios.)

Can it be sold internationally? (For both independents and studios, international sales make up at least sixty percent of the profits.)

Sometimes, even though almost all the above questions are answered "yes," some great scripts never get made. Unfortunately, no one can say if your script will sell or not. Sometimes even the best script doesn't sell due to lack of demand for a particular genre, or because a script was not distributed properly to the right people, or ten scripts in the same genre sold last week.

You should realize that some of the scripts that you write are learning scripts. Part of the evaluation process recognizes that there are ill-conceived ideas, boring stories, and projects that you can't pull off because you don't have the experience. I've worked on more than one first script that would have been fine if it were written by a writer with more experience. The inexperienced writer couldn't pull off the complexities, even with help. Plenty of great writers threw out their first few scripts—for very good reasons. They recognized that sometimes, after years of work, it's time to move on. So the script gets put away. Maybe the writer cries a little, gets a good night's sleep, and goes on. There are always more creative ideas left to explore, new stories pushing at you, characters begging you to bring them to life.

But let's say that one of your scripts sells. Maybe it gets produced. Once it gets made, other evaluations come into play. Does the editor feel it can be stronger by cutting scenes or changing them around? Does the producer insist that ten minutes are cut? Does the composer feel it needs more humor in the music? Do test audiences find some part confusing?

Eventually, it goes out to the audience and the critics. Critics might hate the film and everyone stays away, even though it might be a terrific film. Sometimes audiences and critics love a film, but it's badly distributed and can't compete with studio films with studio marketing dollars behind them. I've worked on two films—*Passtime* and *Picture Bride*—that won rave reviews from critics, won the Audience Favorite Award at Sundance, and were enthusiastically received by audiences. But they were badly distributed with little publicity. Although they played in theaters in Los Angeles and New York and a few other cities, they were never able to find a wider audience.

But, sometimes it all goes right. Your film is released. It brings you fame and fortune and a good feeling for what you've done. You do a bit of celebration, attend your screenings, give a few interviews, receive some awards, go to Cannes and Sundance, take a little trip to rest up. That's all good. But then it's time to move on to the next script, the next story. You're a writer. A writer writes. The creative process continues.

Notes

CHAPTER ONE

1. Thomas Wolfe, "The Story of A Novel," *The Saturday Review Treasury*, John Haverstick, ed. (New York: Simon and Schuster, 1957), p. 69.

2. Arthur Koestler, *The Art of Creation* (New York: Dell Publishing Co., Inc., 1964), p. 89.

3. John A. Glover, Royce R. Ronning, and Cecil R. Reynolds, *Handbook of Creativity: Perspectives on Individual Differences* (New York: Plenum Press, 1989), pp. 233–34.

CHAPTER TWO

1. Mihaly Csikszentmihalyi, *Creativity: Flow and the Psychology of Discovery and Invention* (New York: Harper-Collins Publishers, Inc., 1996), p. 102.

2. John A. Glover, Royce R. Ronning, and Cecil R. Reynolds, *Handbook of Creativity: Perspectives on Individual Differences* (New York: Plenum Press, 1989).

3. Mihaly Csikszentmihalyi, *Creativity: Flow and the Psychology of Discovery and Invention* (New York: Harper-Collins Publishers, Inc., 1996), p. 138.

4. Mihaly Csikszentmihalyi, *Creativity: Flow and the Psychology of Discovery and Invention* (New York: Harper-Collins Publishers, Inc., 1996), pp. 335–36.

5. Natalie Hevener Kaufman and Carol McGinnis Kay (contributor), *G is for Grafton* (New York: Henry Holt & Co. Inc., 1997), p. 278.

6. Ruth Theodos, "William F. Nolan Fires up AWG," *Alameda Writers Group Newsletter*, p. 5.

CHAPTER FOUR

1. For more information about structure, read Chapters Two and Three in *Making a Good Script Great*, 2nd ed., by Linda Seger (Hollywood: Samuel French Trade, 1994).

2. In *The Practice of Poetry: Writing Exercises from Poets Who Teach*, by Robin Behn and Chase Twichell (New York: Harper

Perennial, 1992), p. 73, Lee Upton suggests making up stories from such ideas as "cow pregnant with a space alien's child," "Farmer's wife turns hubby into scarecrow."

CHAPTER SIX

1. *The Practice of Poetry: Writing Exercises from Poets Who Teach*, by Robin Behn and Chase Twichell (New York: Harper Perennial, 1992), pp. 251–53.

2. Ibid, p. 255.

3. *Il Postino* by Anna Pavignano, Michael Radford, Furio Scarpelli, Giacomo Scarpelli, Massimo Troisi.

4. Richard Dyer MacCann, *Film: A Montage of Theories* (New York: E.P. Dutton & Co., Inc., 1966), p. 58.

5. In *The Practice of Poetry: Writing Exercises from Poets Who Teach*, by Robin Behn and Chase Twichell (New York: Harper Perennial, 1992), p. 141, Jack Myers uses a similar exercise with a door, in order to lead readers into using function as metaphor in a poem.

6. In *The Practice of Poetry*, both Christopher Gilbert and Roger Mitchell have created similar exercises, pp. 46 and 68.

CHAPTER SEVEN

1. Joseph Hart, Ph.D., Richard Corriere, Ph.D., Werner Karle, Ph.D., and Lee Woldenberg, Ph.D., *Dreaming and Waking: The Functional Approach to Using Dream* (Los Angeles: The Center Foundation Press, 1980), pp. 36 and 49.

2. Ibid, p. 202.

3. Ibid, p. 189.

4. Ibid, pp. 203–04.

5. Ibid, p. 80 (based on Fritz Perls' techiques, the founder of gestalt therapy).

6. Naomi Epel, *Writers Dreaming* (New York: Vintage Books, 1993), p. 62.

7. Ibid, p. 63.

CHAPTER EIGHT

1. Robert Bly, *A Litle Book on the Human Shadow* (New York: Harper Collins Publishers, 1988), p. 1.

2. Ibid, p. 2.

3. Marsha Scarbrough, "Oh, the Horror! The Genre That Just Won't Die...Allliiiive!," *Written By*, October 1998, p. 27.

4. Ibid.

CHAPTER NINE

1. Albert Rothenberg, M.D., *The Emerging Goddess:The Creative Process in Art, Science, and Other Fields* (Chicago:The University of Chicago Press, 1979), p. 55.

2. Mihaly Csikszentmihalyi lists some of these opposites in *Creativity: Flow and the Psychology of Discovery and Invention* (New York: Harper-Collins Publishers, Inc., 1996), p. 57.

3. *Schindler's List*, screenplay by Steven Zaellian, Universal Studios and Amblin Entertainment, 1993.

4. *Cheers*, Episode #102, "Abnormal Psychology," by Janet Leahy.

CHAPTER ELEVEN

1. Eric Neumann, *Art and the Creative Unconscious* (Princeton: Princeton University Press, 1959), p. 163.

2. Mihaly Csikszentmihalyi, *Creativity: Flow and the Psychology of Discovery and Invention* (New York: Harper-Collins Publishers, 1996), p. 11.

3. From the poem "The Second Coming" by William Butler Yeats.

4. Eric Neumann, *Art and the Creative Unconscious* (Princeton: Princeton University Press, 1959), p. 163.

5. Douglas V. Steere, *Dimensions of Prayer* (London: Libra Books, 1962), p. 68.

Appendix

If you wish to use this book as a companion volume to *Making a Good Script Great*, the following are recommended chapters, plus other suggested books on the topic.

CHAPTER ONE to CHAPTER THREE
Making a Good Script Great—Chapter One: "Gathering Ideas"

If you find it difficult to get started or if you feel blocked, frustrated, afraid, and immobilized, you may find it helpful to read the book *Fearless Creativity* by Eric Maisel.

Among the many excellent books on creativity that would supplement this book:

Blueprint for Writers by Rachel Ballon (particularly Chapter One, "Unlock your Creativity")

The Artist's Way by Julia Cameron

Bird by Bird by Anne Lamott

CHAPTER FOUR
Making a Good Script Great—Chapters Two, Three, Four, and Five.

CHAPTER FIVE
Making a Good Script Great—Chapters Seven and Eight: "Making it Commercial," "Creating the Myth."

For further work on theme, you may want to read:

The Art of Adaptation by Linda Seger—Chapter 7: "Exploring the Theme"

CHAPTER SIX
Making a Good Script Great—Chapter Six: "Creating a Cohesive Script"

The Art of Adaptation—Chapter Eight: "Creating and Shading Style, Mood, and Tone"

The Practice of Poetry, edited by Robin Behn and Chase Twichell. Although written specifically for poets, this book can further broaden the understanding of metaphor.

CHAPTER SEVEN

There are thousands of books about dreams. The ones that shaped my thinking and which I found very accessible:

The Dream Game by Anne Faraday (now out of print but available)

Creative Dreaming by Patricia Garfield

CHAPTER EIGHT

Although there are thousands of books about the shadow, these two I found particularly helpful and accessible for writers.

A Short History of the Shadow by Robert Bly

Romancing the Shadow by Zweig and Wolf

CHAPTER NINE

Making a Good Script Great—Chapters Nine, Ten, Eleven, Twelve: "From Motivation to Goal: Finding the Character Spine," "Finding the Conflict," "Creating Dimensional Characters," "Character Functions"

You may also find it helpful to read *Creating Unforgettable Characters* by Linda Seger.

The Art of Adaptation—Chapter Six: "Choosing the Characters"

CHAPTER TWELVE

If you're ready to market your script, start reading and researching some of the many books about the industry and how to break in. These include:

Opening the Doors to Hollywood by Carlos de Abreu and Howard Jay Smith

Selling Your Screenplay by Cynthia Whitcomb

How to Sell Your Screenplay: The Real Rules of Film and Television by Carl Sautter

The Art, Craft, and Business of Screenwriting by Richard Walter

How to Make It in Hollywood: All The Right Moves by Linda Buzzell

Writing Screenplays That Sell by Michael Hague

Getting Your Script Through the Hollywood Maze: An Insider's Guide by Linda Stuart

Bibliography

Abrams, Jeremiah, and Connie Sweig. *Meeting the Shadow: The Hidden Power of the Dark Side of Nature*. Los Angeles: Jeremy P. Tarcher, Inc., 1991.

Arnheim, Rudolf. *Visual Thinking*. Berkeley, California: University of California Press, 1969.

Atchity, Kenneth and Chi-Li Wong. *Writing Treatments That Sell: How to Create and Market Your Story Ideas to the Motion Picture and TV Industry*. New York: Henry Holt, 1997.

Baker, Paul. *Integration of Abilities: Exercises for Creative Growth*. San Antonio, Texas: Trinity University Press, 1972.

Ballon, Rachel Friedman. *Blueprint for Writing: A Writer's Guide to Creativity, Craft and Career*. Los Angeles: Lowell House, 1994.

Barron, Frank. *Creativity and Personal Freedom*. New York: D. Van Nostrand Company, 1968.

——. *Creative Person and Creative Process*. New York: Holt, Rinehart and Winston, Inc., 1969.

Behn, Robin and Chase Twichell. *The Practice of Poetry: Writing Exercises from Poets Who Teach*. New York: Harper Perennial, 1992.

Berdyaev, Nicholas. *The Meaning of the Creative Act*. New York: Harper & Brothers, 1954.

Bergson, Henri. *The Creative Mind: An Introduction to Metaphysics*. Secaucus, New Jersey: Citadel Press, 1946.

Biondi. Angelo M. *The Creative Process*. Buffalo, New York: D.O.K. Publishers, Inc., 1972.

Bly, Robert. *A Little Book on the Human Shadow*. New York: Harper Collins Publishers, 1988.

Burnham, Sophy. *For Writers Only*. New York: Ballantine Books, 1994.

Buzzell, Linda. *How to Make It in Hollywood: All the Right Moves*. New York: Harper Perennial, 1996.

Cameron, Julie. *The Artists Way: A Spiritual Path to Higher Creativity*. Los Angeles: Jeremy P. Tarcher, 1992.

Campbell, Don. *The Mozart Effect: Tapping the Power of Music to Heal the Body, Strengthen the Mind, and Unlock the Creative Spirit.* New York: Avon Books, 1997.

Csikszentmihalyi, Mihaly. *Creativity: Flow and the Psychology of Discovery and Invention.* New York: Harper-Collins Publishers, Inc., 1996.

de Abreu, Carlos and Howard Jay Smith. *Opening the Doors to Hollywood: How to Sell Your Story, Book, Screenplay Idea.* Los Angeles: Custos Morum Publishers, 1995.

De Bono, Edward. *Serious Creativity: Using the Power of Lateral Thinking to Create New Ideas.* New York: Harper Business, 1992.

Dreistadt, Roy. "The Use of Analogies and Incubation in Obtaining Insights in Creative Problem Solving." *The Journal of Psychology* (1969): 71, 159–175.

Epel, Naomi. *Writers Dreaming.* New York: Vintage Books, 1993.

Egri, Lajos. *The Art of Dramatic Writing.* New York: Simon and Schuster, 1960.

Erlbaum, Lawrence. *Creativity and Divergent Thinking.* Hillsdale, New Jersey: Lawrence, 1993.

Faraday, Ann. *The Dream Game.* New York: Harper and Row Publishers, Inc., 1974.

Feldman, D.H. *Changing the World: A Framework for the Study of Creativity.* Westport, Connecticut: Praeger, 1994.

Freeman, M. *Finding the Muse: A Sociopsycological Inquiry into the Conditions of Artistic Creativity.* New York: Cambridge University Press, 1993.

Friedman, Bonnie. *Writing Past Dark: Envy, Fear, Distraction and Other Dilemmas in the Writer's Life.* New York: Harper-Collins Publishers, Inc., 1993.

Froug, William. *Zen and the Art of Screenwriting: Insights and Interviews.* Los Angeles: Silman-James Press, 1996.

Gallagher, Winifred. *The Power of Place: How Our Surroundings Shape Our Thoughts, Emotions and Actions.* New York: Poseidon Press, 1993.

Gardner, Howard. *Creating Minds: An Anatomy of Creativity Seen Through the Lives of Freud, Einstein, Picasso, Stravinsky, Eliot, Granham and Gandhi.* New York: Basic Books, 1993.

Ghiselin, Brewster. *The Creative Process.* New York: New American Press, 1952.

Glover, John A., Royce R. Ronning, and Cecil R. Reynolds. *Handbook of Creativity: Perspectives on Individual Differences.* New York: Plenum Press, 1989.

Goldberg, Natalie. *Wild Mind: Living the Writer's Life.* New York: Bantam Books, 1990.

Grudin, Robert. *The Grace of Great Things: Creativity and Innovation*. New York: Houghton Mifflin Company, 1990.

Hague, Michael. *Writing Screenplays That Sell*. New York: McGraw-Hill Book Company, 1988.

Harman, Willis, Ph.D., and Howard Rheingold. *Higher Creativity: Liberating the Unconscious for Breakthrough Insights*. New York: Jeremy P. Tarcher/Putnam, 1984.

Hart, Joseph, Ph.D., Richard Corriere, Ph.D., Werner Karle, Ph.D., and Lee Woldenberg, M.D. *Dreaming & Waking: The Functional Approach to Using Dreams*. Los Angeles: The Center Foundation Press, 1980.

Heilbrun, Carolyn G. *Writing a Woman's Life*. New York: Ballantine Books, 1988.

Herbert, Kathryn. *Writing Scripts Hollywood Will Love: An Insider's Guide to Film and Television Scripts That Sell*. New York: Allworth Press, 1994.

Hyde, Lewis. *Trickster Makes This World: Mischief, Myth and Art*. New York: Farrar, Straus and Giroux, 1998.

———. *The Gift: Imagination and the Erotic Life of Property*. New York: Vintage Books, 1983.

Kandinsky, Wassily. *Concerning the Spiritual in Art*. New York: George Wittenborn, Inc., 1947.

Kaufman, Natalie Hevener, and Carol McGinnis Kay (contributor). *The World of Kinsey Millhone*. New York: Henry Holt and Company, 1997.

Keyes, Ralph. *The Courage to Write: How Writers Transcend Fear*. New York: Henry Holt and Company, 1995.

Koestler, Arthur. *The Act of Creation*. New York: Dell Publishing Co., Inc., 1964.

Lamott, Anne. *Bird by Bird: Some Instructions on Writing and Life*. New York: Anchor Books, Doubleday, 1995.

Lee, Philip R., Robert E. Ornstein, David Galin, Arthur Deikman, and Charles T. Tart. *Symposium on Consciousness*. New York: Penguin Books, 1977.

L'Engle, Madeleine. *Walking on Water: Reflections on Faith and Art*. Wheaton, Illinois: Harold Shaw Publishers, 1980.

MacCann, Richard Dyer. *Film: A Montage of Theories*. New York: E.P. Dutton & Co., Inc. 1966.

MacKinnon, Donald W. "The Nature and Nurture of Creative Talent." *American Psychologist*, Vol. 17, 7, 484-495.

Maisel, Eric, Ph.D., *Fearless Creating: A Step-by-step Guide to Starting and Completing Your Work of Art*. New York: Jeremy P. Tarcher/Putnam, 1995.

Maugham, Somerset. *A Writer's Notebook*. New York: Doubleday & Co., 1949.

May, Rollo. *The Courage to Create.* New York: Bantam Books, 1975.

Michalko, Michael. *Thinkertoys:A Handbook of Business Creativity.* Berkeley, California:Ten Speed Press, 1991.

Miller, Peter. *Get Published! Get Produced!:A Literary Agent's Tips on How to Sell Your Writing.* New York: Shapolsky Publishers, 1991.

Moustakas, Clark. *Creativity and Conformity.* New York: D. Van Nostrand Company, 1967.

Nachmanovitch, Stephen. *Free Play: Improvisation in Life and Art.* New York: Jeremy P. Tarcher/Putnam, 1990.

Neumann, Erich. *Art and the Creative Unconscious.* Princeton, New Jersey: Princeton University Press, 1959.

Newman, Lesléa. *Writing from the Heart.* Freedom, California: The Crossing Press, 1993.

Ornstein, Robert E. *The Psychology of Consciousness.* New York: Penguin Books, 1972.

———. *The Nature of Human Consciousness:A Book of Readings.* San Francisco:W.H. Freeman and Company, 1973.

Osborn, Alex F., L.H.D., *Applied Imagination: Principles and Procedures of Creative Problem-Solving.* Buffalo, New York: Creative Education Foundation Press, 1993.

Pinker, Steven. *How the Mind Works.* New York:W.W. Norton & Company, 1997.

Plimpton, George. *The Paris Review Interviews Writers at Work, Fifth Series.* New York:The Viking Press, 1981.

———. *The Paris Review Interviews Writers at Work, Fourth Series.* New York:The Viking Press, 1974.

———. *The Paris Review Interviews Writers at Work, Fourth Series.* New York:The Viking Press, 1984.

Ray, Robert J. *The Weekend Novelist.* New York: Dell Publishing, 1994.

Rothenberg, Albert, M.D. *The Emerging Goddess:The Creative Process in Art, Science, and Other Fields.* Chicago:The University of Chicago Press, 1979.

Runco, M.A. *Divergent Thinking.* Norwood, New Jersey:Ablex, 1991.

Sautter, Carl. *How to Sell Your Screenplay:The Real Rules of Film and Television.* New York: New Chapter Press, 1988.

Scarbrough, Marsha. "Oh, the Horror! The Genre That Just Won't Die ...Allliiiive!" *Written By*, October 1998.

Seger, Linda. *Making a Good Script Great.* Hollywood: Samuel French, 1994.

———. *Creating Unforgettable Characters.* New York: Henry Holt, 1990.

———. *The Art of Adaptation:Turning Fact and Fiction into Film,* New York: Henry Holt, 1992.

———. *From Script to Screen: The Collaborative Art of Filmmaking* (with Edward Whetmore), New York: Henry Holt, 1994.

———. *When Women Call the Shots: The Developing Power and Influence of Women in Television and Film.* New York: Henry Holt, 1996.

Shahn, Ben. *The Shape of Content.* New York: Vintage Books, 1957.

Sternberg, R.J. *The Nature of Creativity: Contemporary Psychological Perspectives.* Cambridge, England: Cambridge Univerity Press, 1988.

———. and J.E. Stevenson. *The Nature of Insight.* Cambridge: Cambridge University Press, 1995.

Steere, Douglas V. *Dimensions of Prayer.* London: Libra Books, 1962.

Storr, Anthony. *Solitude: A Return to the Self.* New York: Ballantine Books, 1988.

Stuart, Linda. *Getting Your Script through the Hollywood Maze: An Insider's Guide.* Venice, California: Acrobat Books, 1993.

Theodos, Ruth. "William F. Nolan Fires up AWG." *Alameda Writers Group Newsletter.*

Trottier, David. *The Screenwriter's Bible: A Complete Guide to Writing, Formatting, and Selling Your Script* (3rd Ed). Los Angeles: Silman-James Press, 1998.

Vance, Mike, and Diane Deacon. *Think Out of the Box.* Franklin Lakes, New Jersey: Career Press, 1997.

Vernon, P.E. *Creativity.* Middlesex, England: Penguin Books, Ltd., 1970.

Vogler, Christopher. *The Writer's Journey: Mythic Structure for Storytellers and Screenwriters.* Studio City, California: Michael Wiese Productions, 1996.

von Oech, Roger. *A Whack on the Side of the Head: How You Can Be More Creative.* New York: Warner Books, Inc., 1998.

Walter, Richard. *The Art, Craft and Business of Screenplay Writing.* New York: Plume, 1988.

Whitcomb, Cynthia. *Selling Your Screenplay.* New York: Crown, 1988.

Wycoff, Joyce. *Mindmapping: Your Personal Guide to Exploring Creativity and Problem-Solving.* New York: Berkley Books, 1991.

Zweig, Connie, Ph.D., and Steve Wolf, Ph.D. *Romancing the Shadow: Illuminating the Dark Side of the Soul.* New York: Ballantine Books, 1997.